"In the center sat Coyote"

IN THE
REIGN OF COYOTE

FOLKLORE FROM THE PACIFIC COAST

BY

KATHERINE CHANDLER

AUTHOR OF "HABITS OF CALIFORNIA PLANTS" AND ' THE BIRD
WOMAN OF THE LEWIS AND CLARK EXPEDITION"

DRAWINGS BY

J W FERGUSON KENNEDY

Fredonia Books
Amsterdam, The Netherlands

In the Reign of Coyote

by
Katherine Chandler

ISBN: 1-58963-431-4

Copyright © 2001 by Fredonia Books

Reprinted from the 1905 edition

Fredonia Books
Amsterdam, The Netherlands
http://www.fredoniabooks.com

In order to make original editions of historical works
available to scholars at an economical price, this
facsimile of the original edition of 1905 is
reproduced from the best available copy and has
been digitally enhanced to improve legibility, but the
text remains unaltered to retain historical
authenticity.

TO MY BROTHER

ALBERT E CHANDLER

WHOSE STEADFAST SYMPATHY HAS MADE POSSIBLE

THIS COLLECTION OF FOLKLORE

PREFACE

Some of the tales contained in this book have already been published in the San Francisco *Chronicle*, Los Angeles *Times, Sunset, Popular Educator, Children's World*, and *Good Housekeeping*

The stories from Lower California, as related by Tecla, were told to me by Mrs Jules Simoneau of Monterey, California, who is an Indian from Mazatlan   The sources of those chapters containing stories of Alta California are as follows   "Old Deer and Old Grizzly," Albert Samuel Gatschet in *The United States Geographical and Geological Survey of the Rocky Mountain Region Contributions to North American Ethnology*, II, Part I, 118, "Why the Coyote is so Cunning," Stephen Powers, III, 35, "How the Animals secured Fire," 38, "Coyote's Ride on a Star," 39, "How the Animals secured Light," 182, "Why the Bat is Blind," 343, "The Creation of Man," 358, "The Creation of the World," 273, and J Owen Dorsey in *The American Anthropologist*, II, 38, "The Story of the Pleiades," Alexander S Taylor in *The California Farmer*, "Indianology of California," January

18, 1861. The Oregon country represented by
Klayukat's tales is meant to include the vast un-
bounded territory known by that name previous to
1848. The material for the stories was garnered
from the following books: "How the Animals got
their Colors," Franz Boas, *Bureau of American
Ethnology: Kathlamet Texts, Bulletin* 26, 39;
"Why there is only One Southwest Wind," 67;
"The Robin and the Salmon Berry," 118; "Why
the Owl eats only Small Creatures," *The Pacific
Northwest Oregon and Washington,* 2 vols., com-
piled and published by the Northwest Pacific His-
tory Company, Portland, Oregon, 1889, II, 66;
"The Subjugation of the Thunderbird," 67;
"How the Animals secured Salmon," 68; "Why
the Tick is now Small," 69; "The Frog in the
Moon," 70; "Why the Sun travels regularly," 70;
"Why the Mosquito hates Smoke," 74; "Why the
Snakes change their Skins," 76; "Why the Dead
do not come back," 80.

While the essentials of the stories have been
retained, the narratives have been elaborated and
modified.

The setting of three Indians from different tribes
on the same Californian ranch is historically true.
Indian servants from Mexico and Lower California
accompanied the pioneers northward; the California

Indians who were taught trades at the Missions often drifted into the service of the families , and the records of San Carlos Mission show that on November 14, 1791, seventeen natives of "*Puerto de San Lorenzo de Nutka en el Estrechos de San Juan de Fuca*" were baptized into the Holy Catholic Church at that Mission

I am indebted to Miss Harriet Hawley of New York for criticism both of the spirit and the technique of these stories, and to my sister, Mabel G Chandler, for assistance in correction

KATHERINE CHANDLER

SAN FRANCISCO, CALIFORNIA
    May, 1905

CONTENTS

PAGE

THE FROG AND THE COYOTE 3

THE CREATION OF THE WORLD 7

HOW THE ANIMALS SECURED LIGHT 14

THE BIG FROG AND THE LITTLE FROGS 21

HOW THE ANIMALS SECURED FIRE 24

THE ANT AND THE SNOW 31

THE CRICKET AND THE COUGAR 34

WHY THE MOSQUITO HATES SMOKE 38

WHY THE SNAKES CHANGE THEIR SKINS 43

WHY THERE IS ONLY ONE SOUTHWEST WIND . . 47

THE FOX AND THE COYOTE 56

THE FROG IN THE MOON 59

HOW THE ANIMALS GOT THEIR COLORS 63

THE RACCOON AND THE MAN-OF-TAR 70

OLD DEER AND OLD GRIZZLY 76

	PAGE
THE ROBIN AND THE SALMON BERRY	85
HOW THE ANIMALS SECURED SALMON	95
WHY THE TICK IS NOW SMALL	100
WHY THE SUN TRAVELS REGULARLY	105
THE SUBJUGATION OF THE THUNDERBIRD	109
WHY THE BAT IS BLIND	114
WHY THE OWL EATS ONLY SMALL CREATURES	118
WHY THE DEAD DO NOT COME BACK	125
COYOTE'S RIDE ON A STAR	132
THE CREATION OF MAN	136
WHY THE COYOTE IS SO CUNNING	142
THE STORY OF THE PLEIADES	148
GLOSSARY OF CALIFORNIA TERMS	157
INDEX	159

IN THE REIGN OF COYOTE

THE FROG AND THE COYOTE

WHEN Doña Juanita was a tiny girl like you, Mabel, and Don Antonio was a little boy like you, Joe, they lived on a large ranch across the bay from San Francisco. They had no school to attend, and they saw other white children only at Christmas, or Easter, or Saint Francis' Day, or some other such great feast time. They had their lessons, of course, — book lessons, which were not long enough to weary them; riding lessons, which carried them over the hills many hours a day; and music lessons, which consisted in practicing guitar and violin accompaniments to the sweet old Spanish songs. In addition, Juanita was taught all kinds of needlework, from plain hemming to the finest embroidery. As for amusements, they played dancing games with each other and with the children of the Indian servants, and they listened

3

to the stories that Tecla, their nurse, old Klayukat, the saddler, and Wantasson, the blacksmith, delighted to tell.

There was a rivalry among these three storytellers, for they came from different tribes, and the legends of their people were not the same.

Tecla was from Baja, or Lower, California, where Juanita and Antonio's mother had once lived. Old Klayukat's tribal home was to the far north, at Puget Sound. He had been brought down by a king's vessel and given into the charge of the padres at the mission of San Francisco d'Assisi. There he had become a Christian and had been taught the saddler's trade. He had been employed by the children's grandfather ever since their father was a little boy. Wantasson was from Alta California, which is the California that now belongs to the United States. Before he had become Christianized at the mission, he had wandered about and so knew stories from the different tribes of the country.

To Juanita and Antonio it mattered little from what places the stories came,—whether from the northern Oregon Country, Baja California, or their own Alta California. All the tales were fascinating to them, and they were always eager to do any favor for Wantasson, Klayukat, or Tecla in the hope of winning a story in return.

One hot day the children and Tecla were lying under the big oak tree by the spring, when they saw a small green frog hop among the little yellow water flowers which we call "brass buttons."

"Did I ever tell you the story of the frog and the coyote?" asked Tecla.

"Oh, no; please tell it now"; and Juanita clapped her hands.

"Do tell it, my good Tecla," added Antonio. (Spanish Californian children were trained to be always polite to their elders, no matter what social position these occupied.)

"Well, sit still, thou restless Nita, and I will tell it as my godfather told it to me."

———

One day the coyote found a frog in the road, and said, "Now, I shall eat you up."

The frog replied: "Oh, don't eat me to-day, Brother Coyote. Let us run a race to-morrow, and if you win, then you may eat me."

The coyote said, "All right."

Then the frog went to see his frog friends, and said, "I am going to run a race with the coyote to-morrow, from the spring to the elder tree and back, and if he wins, he is to eat me."

"Ha, ha! Of course he will win," laughed his friends.

"Not if you will help me, as friends should," said the frog. "One of you go to the turning stake and, when you see the coyote coming, give three jumps to show him that you are ahead. I will stay near the home stake and jump in ahead of him when he is coming back." The frog's friends agreed to help him.

The next day the coyote came to run the race. The frog was there, and at the appointed time they both started, but the frog gave only three jumps and then lay down on the grass to rest. The coyote ran very fast; and, as he did not see the frog, he thought him far behind. As he neared the turning post, he saw the frog jump three times in front of him.

"Oh, this is strange," said the coyote; "I did not see you pass me. But I will beat you home."

He ran as fast as he could, but when he came in sight of the home stake, there was the frog making the three last jumps.

Then the coyote ran away in disgust.

"The frog was not a gentleman," commented Antonio, "for he was acting a lie."

"Your Señora Madre calls," said Tecla; "we must go to her. God willing, to-morrow I will tell you about another frog, — and he was not a gentleman either."

THE CREATION OF THE
WORLD

LATER that afternoon Antonio wandered to the blacksmith's shop. Wantasson was hammering a wheel tire into shape.

"Well, young Antonio, have you minded the heat this day?" he inquired, as he wiped his forehead with his sleeve.

"Oh, no, Wantasson; we have been down by the spring where it is always cool. And Tecla told us a new story. It was about the frog that raced with the coyote and won the race by acting a lie."

"Ugh! That woman Tecla does not get her stories straight. How could a frog lie to Coyote? Coyote would know it. Why, Coyote is the most cunning of all the animals. And all the other animals know it. If it had n't been for Coyote there would n't be any other animals, or any world, or any you, or any me, or any Tecla to tell such false stories. Now would there, young Antonio?"

"Would n't there be *anything* without Coyote, Wantasson?"

"No, nothing; not even that sunflower against the fence. You know Coyote made the world, don't you?"

"Coyote?" Into Antonio's mind flashed the words he had learned in his catechism, " *God made the world* "; but his desire for the story brushed them aside for the moment. "Will you tell me how he made it, Wantasson?"

"Yes. Wait until I put this tire to cool; then I will rest awhile and tell it to you."

Antonio made a trumpet of his hands and shouted: "Nita, Nita, come here. Wantasson will tell us a story."

Juanita came hurrying, and soon the children were sitting in the shadow in front of the smithy, listening to Wantasson's story.

———

In the beginning of things it was all dark and still. There was no wind and neither was there any rain. There was no world as we see it to-day.

All was water except for one little point of rock. On this rock lived Coyote and Eagle, and they were the only living things in the world.

Coyote lay on the rock thinking. After a long time he said to Eagle, "Sister Eagle, go to the edge of the rock and watch to see if anything happens."

In a little while Eagle called out, "O Brother Coyote, far to the north I see a tree rising out of the water."

"Very good," answered Coyote. "That tree shall be the *ash*, and all people shall esteem it for all time. Watch again, Sister Eagle, and see what now happens."

After a time Eagle again raised her voice. "Look to the south, Brother Coyote. There is another tree peeping up out of the water."

"Very good," answered Coyote. "That tree shall be the *cedar*. Throughout all ages all people shall delight in its breath. Watch again, Sister Eagle, and see what next appears."

Presently Eagle announced: "Look to the southwest, Brother Coyote. Something strange and red comes out of the water there."

"Ah!" exclaimed Coyote, "that must be land." He rose to his feet and gazed toward the southwest.

A red mass was slowly approaching the place where he stood. It floated up until it touched the point of rock. It was land, but it was shaking like a jellyfish. Coyote pressed it with his paws to steady it. When it had become solid and still, he looked over it.

"This is not enough land," he muttered; "we must have more."

He picked up three pieces of rock and two clumps of earth. He threw one piece of rock and then listened as it sank down, down into the depths of the water. He threw a second piece of rock and again listened as it went down, down through the water and struck the first rock lying at the bottom.

"Very good," he laughed. "Now, third rock, go and rest upon the other two."

He threw the third rock and listened as it sank down, down through the water and settled on top of the second rock. Then he threw in the two clumps of earth, one at a time, and when the last struck the water, land appeared at the surface. Then the water began to dash in great waves and to embrace the land and to withdraw from it.

"Very good," said Coyote. "Thus shall the water always act, and people for all time shall call its movements the *tides*." That is why we have tides to-day, because Coyote said it should be so.

Coyote looked over the land and saw great dents on its surface. "Those do not please me," he said. "They mean sickness. Water, come up and cover over the land again."

The water swirled and hurled itself all over the land. Then Coyote blew softly, saying the while, "Land, come up again."

The land returned. It still had great dents on its surface. "What! still sickness!" exclaimed Coyote. "This must not be. Water, cover over the land again."

Again the water swirled and whirled and covered the land. Once more Coyote blew softly on it and said, "Land, come up again."

The land reappeared, but again its surface had dents upon it. "Sickness yet!" and Coyote became angry. "Sickness shall not remain upon the land. Water, cover over the land again."

The water did as it was bidden, but when Coyote called up the land again, its surface was dented as before. He ordered it under water once more; but for the fifth time it remained unchanged.

Then, indeed, Coyote's anger was great. "I will try no more," he cried. "As the land has chosen sickness, sickness it shall have for all time." That is why we have sickness to-day, because Coyote said it should be so.

When Eagle looked over the land and saw that it was flat, she said, "There is no place for me to perch."

"That is easily changed," replied Coyote; and he rounded up some little hills.

"Huh! those are only footstools," objected Eagle. "I must have lofty cliffs for my perch."

"Well, then, Sister Eagle, make better ones to suit yourself," returned Coyote.

"Thank you, I will," answered Eagle; and she set to work. She dug her claws into the earth and scratched up some mountains. As she worked hard over the task, some of her feathers fell out and rooted in the earth. The long feathers became trees, — pines, firs, redwoods, and the other tall trees; the pinfeathers grew into manzanita and coffee berry and chaparral and similar shrubs; while the down from her breast brought forth poppies and baby-blue-eyes and buttercups and all the little flowering plants.

"Very good," said Coyote. Then he took two hairs from his body. One he threw into the water and the other upon the land. They both wriggled about and writhed themselves out into two great Serpents. The one in the water coiled itself around the land five times, so as to hold the earth together. The Land Serpent twisted itself up into one of those dents which Coyote could not remove and breathed out storms through its fiery nostrils.

Then Coyote pulled out two other hairs from his body and threw them upon the land. They bunched themselves into a roll and then waggled themselves into two Dogs.

After that Coyote made Grizzly, Cougar, Antelope, Beaver, and all the other animals. He made that day two of every kind of animal that is now on the earth. And everything he said that day still holds as a law. We still have earth on the top of the land and rock underneath, because Coyote threw the rocks into the water first, and then the earth. All of Coyote's laws still hold to-day.

"And if there had n't been any dents, Wantasson, would n't we have the measles and have to drink tansy tea?" A recent siege was fresh in Juanita's memory.

"But *what* made the dents, Wantasson?" interrupted Antonio. "What made them when Coyote did n't want them?"

"You ask too many questions, young Antonio. Look at the dents in that wheel tire. They came there and *I* did n't want them. I 've got to heat it again and straighten those out." And not another word could the children win from him that afternoon.

HOW THE ANIMALS SECURED LIGHT

AFTER breakfast the next morning Antonio and Juanita were each given two nectarines to eat in the garden.

"Let's eat only one ourselves and take the others to Wantasson," suggested Antonio. "He didn't feel well yesterday afternoon."

"Let's," agreed Juanita. "Then perhaps he'll become good-natured and tell us another story."

"Well, don't ask any questions at the end and make him cross again."

"Don't ask questions yourself. Your question was what made him angry."

14

"But it was what you said that made me think of the dents. Sh —! Wantasson will hear us." As they were talking, they had skipped across the quadrangle to the smithy.

"Good morning, Wantasson; we've brought you some nectarines, some that came from Santa Clara yesterday," said Juanita.

No work could be so important as eating nectarines. Wantasson sat down in the sunny doorway to devour the fruit. The children stood in the shade inside.

"You like the bright sunshine, don't you, Wantasson?" volunteered Juanita.

"Yes, child, I like the sunshine. I get as much of it as I can, for I remember that once the earth had no sun and no light, and I don't like to get into those ways."

"How did the earth get the sun? We should like to know about that," said Antonio.

"Yes, please tell us," added Juanita.

"It was because of Coyote. You will see that Coyote has much sense and is not easily fooled, as that woman Tecla tells you. Coyote is a very cunning animal."

The children waited eagerly until Wantasson settled his shoulders against the door jamb and began his story.

In the early days the earth was wrapped in darkness. The animals could not see more than a step in front of them. They were always bumping into each other, and they had bruises all over their bodies. Their limbs were growing stiff through lack of exercise; yet no one dared to run for fear of colliding with some other animal. They just groped about with staring eyes, trying to see what was ahead of them.

One day Coyote was thinking hard as he walked and forgot to peer into the darkness. Suddenly his head banged into somebody moving fast toward him. He fell back and saw lights dancing up and down before his eyes.

"*Caw-hou!*" came Hawk's voice. "My head is split. Oh, this terrible darkness! I wish we had some way of seeing how to get about. Oh, my poor head is split!"

"And my poor head, too," rejoined Coyote. "You're not hurt worse than I. Lights are dancing up and down before my eyes."

"Is that you, Coyote? You can't be hurt so much as I, for you are heavier. If you have lights dancing before you, why don't you catch them and hang them up to give us all light?"

"The lights are gone now," answered Coyote, "but your thought is a wise one. Let us see what we can do."

He thought for a long time. Then he said, "Wait here for me."

He groped his way down to a swamp and gathered a bunch of dry tules. He picked up a piece of flint and wrapped the tules around it, making a ball. Then he groped his way back to the waiting Hawk.

"Here, Sister Hawk, take this in your bill and fly as high as you can. When you are too tired to go further, give it a twist and throw it up higher. As you toss it, say, 'Give us light, O Tules. Deliver us from darkness, O Flint.' Then you may come back."

"All right," answered Hawk, and she flew, and flew, and flew, straight up into the darkness, until her wings could not lift her body one stroke more. Then she gave the ball a twist and threw it above her. "Give us light, O Tules. Deliver us from darkness, O Flint," she murmured in a faint voice.

The ball spun upward. As it left her bill, it grew bright. It sent out more and more light as it sped, until finally it became the great golden Sun. Hawk's eyes were blinded. She drooped her head upon her breast and sank down to the earth.

There the animals were all sitting still in amazement. They covered their eyes with their paws. They did not know what to do. After a while

"Hawk flew straight up into the darkness"

Coyote said: "You grumbled over the darkness. Now I have given you light. We will call this light the *sun*. Henceforth no animal shall bump into his brother, and you will no longer suffer from bruises."

Turning to Hawk, Coyote continued: "You have done well, Sister Hawk. Let us do more. Let us make another sun so that this sun can rest sometimes."

"All right," answered Hawk.

Coyote ran to the swamp and hastily gathered an armful of tules. He took a piece of flint for a center and wound the tules into a ball. Then he sped back to Hawk.

"You need not fly so high this time, Sister Hawk, but take it far enough away from the world so that it will not burn us."

"Very well," answered Hawk ; and she flew and flew, straight up, until she was tired. Then she rested a moment. As she cast the ball from her, she murmured, "Give us light, O Tules. Deliver us from darkness, O Flint."

Now Coyote had hurried so at the swamp the second time that he gathered damp tules. Therefore this second ball did not give out a bright golden light as the other did, but sent down pale silver rays.

Coyote looked at it. "It is not very bright," he muttered, "but it will be better than the darkness. We will call it the *moon*, and it shall be in the sky to show us our way when the sun gets tired."

"I should think the moon —" began Juañita, when Antonio raised his voice above hers with "That's a fine story, Wantasson. Coyote did have a lot of sense, didn't he?"

"Yes, Coyote has sense, but you children must run away now. I must make another tire, or your Señor Padre will say that I don't work enough, as he did yesterday."

THE BIG FROG AND THE
LITTLE FROGS

THAT afternoon, as Tecla was dressing the children after their siesta, they clamored for the other frog story.

"Tell it to us now, please, Tecla."

"Impatient ones! Shall I waste the little breath this hot sun leaves me? No, no; let us go to the spring first, and then if you are good, we will see what I can remember."

When they were settled in the oak's cool shade, she told them the promised story.

———

Once there was a long, long rain, and all the ground was wet. Three little frogs crept into a hole to keep themselves dry. After a while a big frog came along, looked in, and said, "Come, come, what are you doing in there?"

"We came in here so that we shouldn't get drowned," answered the little frogs.

"I don't want to get drowned, either; so let me in, too."

"Well, come in, Big Frog"; and they huddled together to make room for him.

The big frog came in. In a little while he took a big breath and puffed out his sides.

The little frogs all cried, "Oh, don't do that. You are squeezing us."

The big frog said nothing, but after a while he again took a long breath and puffed out his sides still more.

Then the little frogs cried, "Oh, oh! you are squeezing us so that we can't stand it."

The big frog answered, "Well, if you don't like it in here, Young Frogs, you'd better get out"; and he took another big breath and squeezed the little frogs so hard that they were pushed out into the cold rain.

———

"And did the poor little frogs have to stay out in the rain all day?" asked Juanita.

"Oh, that didn't hurt them!" answered her brother. "Frogs are always crying for rain, and when it doesn't come they find a creek or a spring. See that one now in the brass buttons. Just watch me hit him." But Antonio's carefully aimed acorn missed the shining little green coat.

"O Tonio!" began Juanita, when Tecla frightened away her words by exclaiming, "See that little black ant on your skirt, Nita. I wonder if he is coming from the blacksmith's."

"From the blacksmith's? From Wantasson's? Why would an ant be at a blacksmith's?"

"I know one ant that went to a blacksmith, and it was fortunate for him that he did. My godfather told me about him."

"Oh, tell us about it, Tecla! Tell it just the way your godfather told it to you."

"No more to-day. To-morrow I will tell you, but now you can ask your blacksmith for a story. I shall take a nap here. I have to rest some time."

Finding it hopeless to persuade her, the children wandered back to the quadrangle.

HOW THE ANIMALS
SECURED FIRE

AT the smithy Antonio and Juanita found Wantasson hard at work. As he saw them, he dropped his tools and sat down in the doorway. He was evidently glad of an excuse to rest, so Antonio made good use of the opportunity.

"Wantasson, do you know a good story about a frog?"

"A good story about a frog?" The words came slowly. "Well, I know a story about a good frog. Would you like to hear it?"

"Yes; that's why we came," explained Juanita, as she and her brother settled themselves on the stones in front of the door.

Wantasson grunted a moment, found a comfortable position for his shoulders, and then began his tale.

———

A long, long time ago all the fire on the earth was owned by two old women. They kept it in a little mat house and would not let a spark escape. The animal people were shivering with cold and were sick from their raw food, so they journeyed two moons to the little mat house and begged the old women to give them a firebrand.

But the old women only muttered, "No, no," and crouched closer to their fire.

Then the animals begged earnestly: "Oh, lend us a brand just for a few minutes. Our teeth are chattering, and our stomachs refuse the uncooked meat. We pray you, Old Women, lend us a firebrand."

But the old women still muttered, "No, no," and hugged their fire closer.

Then the animals piled all their treasures together, — shells from the seashore, cones from the mountains, bows from the oak tree, and arrows from the volcanic region. They carried them to the old women's door. "Old Women," they cried, "here are all our treasures. Take them and give us one burning fagot."

Still the old women muttered, "No, no," and covered their fire with their stooping bodies.

The animals went shivering home. They found Coyote and besought him to think of some way to get them fire.

Coyote thought and thought. Then he said : "It will be a hard struggle to get it safe to our own country. Summon every animal and then station yourselves along the route to the old women's house, each one a half sun's distance from the other. The strongest and swiftest must stand nearest the little mat house. Let each one be ready to run swiftly in his turn with the firebrand. Bear will hide himself outside the old women's home. I will go in. When I signal to him, he will make a rush and frighten them."

Coyote went to the little mat house and knocked at the door. The old women opened it. "Good morning," said Coyote in his politest voice. "May I come in and warm my feet ? They are very cold."

The old women muttered, "Yes, yes."

When Coyote's toes were all flexible again, he coughed. Bear rushed in with a growl and dashed toward the old women. As they tried to protect themselves, Coyote snatched a blazing brand and fled.

But the old women were swift of foot, and as Coyote ran on with lolling tongue and panting breath, they sped after him. Just as he was beginning to slacken his pace, he reached Panther.

Panther seized the brand and bounded onward. The old women followed close. As Panther began

"Bear will hide himself outside the old women's home"

to get weary, he arrived at Elk's station. Elk speeded like the wind, but still the old women followed close behind. Then Fox carried the stolen fire on a space, and so in turn the animals kept up their flight, with the old women always close behind.

At last the firebrand had been carried from one animal to another across the cold country until bushy-tailed Squirrel was reached, and he was the next-to-the-last animal. As he seized the brand, the old women made a dash at him. He was so frightened that he almost dropped it, and in catching it firmly again, his tail caught fire. He did not stop, but ran on with the brand in his mouth. He curled his tail over his back, and it burned a black place between his shoulders. Down to this very day the squirrel has a black spot between his shoulders.

When Squirrel could run no more, he tossed the brand to the last animal in the line. This was poor little squatty Frog. He never was much of a runner, but he did his best, hopping frantically along. The rough stones cut all his tail away; yet he managed to reach the bank of the river, on the other side of which lay the animals' country. Here the old women overtook him and tried to snatch both the brand and poor Frog. The brand had dwindled down to a tiny spark during this long race, so Frog just swallowed it and dived into the river. He swam under water to the other side and there spat out the fire on pieces of wood.

Poor Frog ! He suffered in the struggle. Never since that day has his tail grown again. Then, too, the brand burned away one of his vocal chords, so that he no longer rivals the birds as he once did. That is why he dislikes fire and even to this day keeps far away from it.

From that time fire has dwelt in wood, and by rubbing two twigs together the animals can always get enough to make themselves comfortable.

"Oh, what a good frog !" exclaimed Juanita.

"Yes, he's a brave fellow," assented Antonio. "But can you always get fire out of wood by rubbing two sticks together, Wantasson ? If I should rub these two pieces of wood, would I get fire ?" and he picked up two pieces of firewood.

"*You* probably would not. But my people start all their fires by twirling wood. Some day I may show you how. But now I see your Señor Padre coming, and I must ask him about this work. You go to that woman Tecla."

As they went off, Juanita exclaimed : "I don't care if frogs don't have tails. And I don't think their voices are so bad. *Pobrecito*, to have his vocal chord burned away! How it must have hurt !"

"I know it hurt. I remember when I drank the boiling coffee at old Santo's. It just made my mouth open, it burned so. Perhaps that's why my voice is not so high as yours, Nita. You never drank boiling coffee."

THE ANT AND THE SNOW

THE next day, after their siesta, the children would not give Tecla any peace until she had told them the ant story she had promised.

———

Once a little ant was out walking, and some snow fell and hurt its leg.

"Oh, oh!" he cried; "my poor leg!"

"What's the matter?" asked the snow.

"Oh! I have hurt my leg. Can you help me?"

"I cannot," said the snow. "Ask the sun. It is stronger than I, for it melts me."

So the ant went to the sun and said, "O Sun, I have hurt my leg. Will you help me?"

"I cannot," said the sun. "Ask the cloud. It is stronger than I, for it covers me."

Then the ant went to the cloud. "O Cloud, I have hurt my leg. Will you help me?"

"I cannot," said the cloud. "Ask the wind. It is stronger than I, for it blows me across the sky."

The ant went to the wind and said, "O Wind, I have hurt my leg. Will you help me?"

"I cannot," said the wind. "Ask the adobe. It is stronger than I, for it stops me."

Then the ant went to the adobe. "O Adobe, I have hurt my leg. Will you help me?"

"I cannot," said the adobe. "Ask the mouse. It is stronger than I, for it makes holes in me."

So the ant went to the mouse and said, "O Mouse, I have hurt my leg. Will you help me?"

"I cannot," said the mouse. "Ask the cat. It is stronger than I, for it eats mice."

The ant went to the cat. "O Cat, I have hurt my leg. Will you help me?"

"I cannot," said the cat. "Ask the dog. It is stronger than I, for it worries me."

So the ant went to the dog and said, "O Dog, I have hurt my leg. Will you help me?"

"I cannot," said the dog. "Ask the stick. It is stronger than I, for it beats me."

The ant went to the stick and said, "O Stick, I have hurt my leg. Will you help me?"

"I cannot," said the stick. "Ask the fire. It is stronger than I, for it burns me."

Then the ant went to the fire. " O Fire, I have hurt my leg. Will you help me?"

" I cannot," said the fire. "Ask the water. It is stronger than I, for it quenches me."

The ant went to the water and said, " O Water, I have hurt my leg. Will you help me?"

" I cannot," said the water. "Ask the ox. It is stronger than I, for it drinks me."

Then the ant went to the ox and said, " O Ox, I have hurt my leg. Will you help me?"

" I cannot," said the ox. "Ask the knife. It is stronger than I, for it kills oxen."

Then the ant went to the knife. " O Knife, I have hurt my leg. Will you help me?"

" I cannot," said the knife. "Ask the black-smith. He is stronger than I, for he made me."

So the ant went to the blacksmith and said, " O Blacksmith, I have hurt my leg. Will you help me?"

And the blacksmith took a tiny piece of hemp and bound up the leg, and the little ant crawled away home happy.

" Well, I 'm glad the poor ant got its leg fixed at last," said Juanita.

" I 'll show you that my legs are stronger than yours, Nita, by racing you to the house "; and the children were soon flying up the hill, with Tecla following leisurely after them.

THE CRICKET AND THE
COUGAR

ONE day Juanita and Tecla were sewing in the courtyard, while Antonio lay on his back near their feet watching a humming bird dart in and out of the trumpet flowers. Suddenly Antonio turned over and raised himself to a sitting position. "I wish these ants would let a person enjoy his own yard," he grumbled.

That gave Juanita a thought. "Tecla, do you know any more stories about the ant?" she asked.

"No more about the ant, but I know one about his cousin, the cricket. My godmother told it to me when I was smaller than you, Nita. If you will keep on with your seam and not waste your time, I will tell you that story now."

Juanita straightened herself up in her chair and smoothed out her towel. Then, as she drew her needle in and out, Tecla told them the story.

One day the cougar was out walking in the woods. As he was stepping near an old rotten log, he heard a tiny voice say, "Oh, please don't step there. That's my house, and with one step more you will destroy it."

The cougar looked down and saw a little cricket sitting on the log. He roared, "And is it you, weak little creature, that dares to tell me where to step? Don't you know that I am king of the beasts?"

"You may be king of the beasts, but I am king of my house, and I don't want you to break it down, king or no king."

The cougar was amazed at such daring. "Don't you know, you weakling, that I could kill you and your house and all your relatives with one blow of my paw?"

"I may be weak, but I have a cousin no bigger than I am, who can master you in a fight."

"O-ho! o-ho!" laughed the cougar. "Well, little boaster, you have that cousin here to-morrow; and if he does not master me, I'll crush you, and your house, and your cousin all together."

"The next day the cougar came back to the same spot"

The next day the cougar came back to the same spot and roared, "Now, boaster, bring on your valiant cousin."

Pretty soon he heard a buzzing near his ear. Then he felt a stinging. "Oh, oh!" he roared, "get out of my ear!" But the cricket's cousin, the mosquito, kept on singing and stinging.

With every sting the cougar roared louder and scratched his ear and jumped around; but the mosquito kept on stinging and singing.

The cricket sat on the log and looked on. At last he said, "Mr. Cougar, are you satisfied to leave my house alone?"

"Yes, anything, anything," groaned the cougar, "if you will only get your cousin out of my ear."

So the cricket called the mosquito off, and then the cougar ran away and never bothered them any more.

"Once a flea got into my ear," broke in Antonio, eagerly, "and I was almost crazy until mamma put some warm oil in and drowned the flea out."

"Yes, I can remember how you cried," said his sister.

"No, you can't. You were too little then. And you'd cry, too, with a flea thundering in your ear."

"You may put up your sewing now, Nita," said Tecla, "and play until supper time."

WHY THE MOSQUITO
HATES SMOKE

THAT same day the children were passing the saddler's shop, where Klayukat sat on a whalebone by the door braiding a lariat. As he answered their greeting, he raised his hand to kill a mosquito on his forehead. "You vile mosquito!" he exclaimed; "I wish I could treat you as Coyote did your ancestor."

The children stopped short. "How was that? What did Coyote do to the mosquito?" asked Antonio.

"Tecla told us about the cougar and the mosquito," interjected Juanita, "but not about the coyote. Please tell us about it, Klayukat."

"Huh! Tecla! That woman does not know about Coyote. I don't know what they have in her

country. You ask Wantasson if Coyote is not the
most cunning of the animals."

"Wantasson has told us so. But he did not tell us
about Coyote and the mosquito. Please tell us that,
Klayukat," and Antonio's voice dropped into its
most pleading tones.

"Wait until I get some more leather, and then
as I braid the lariat I will tell you the story."

The children seated themselves near his doorway. Soon he returned and sat down on his whalebone. Then he commenced his work and his story
at the same time.

In the long, long ago Mosquito was larger than
any man now alive. His bill was five feet long, and
it ended in a strong sharp point. He lived in a
narrow canyon near a spring.

When any animal came for water, Mosquito
would rush out singing, "Now I'll suck you, suck,
suck." He would stick his bill through the animal
and drink every drop of blood in its body. So
many did he kill that there was weeping in each
animal home, and every family begged Coyote to
find them relief.

Coyote thought long and deep. Then he took
his stone knife and five twigs, — one of hazel, one
of elder, one of crab apple, one of pine, and one of

oak. With these he started to the canyon where lived Mosquito.

As he approached the door, Mosquito buzzed out in a very annoying manner: "Where are you going? This is my road. I don't allow any one to pass."

Before he could get his bill out of his house, Coyote answered in his polite way: "My friend, I see that you are very cold and have no fire in your house. Let me make you a fire so that you can warm yourself."

Mosquito was feeling a little sluggish, and the ground looked damp, so he replied, "Well, make a little fire, but don't be too long about it or I might get hungry."

Coyote took the hazel twig and broke it in two. He twirled the pieces together and twirled them again, but no blaze came. "Bah!" he exclaimed, "do you send all your heat into your nuts, foolish wood?" and he threw the hazel aside.

Next he took the elder twig and broke it in two. He twirled the pieces together long and rapidly and yet no spark was emitted. "Bah!" he cried, "do you send all your heat to your berries, foolish wood?" and he cast the elder aside.

Then he took the twig of crab apple and broke it in two. He twirled and twirled these pieces together, but they showed no sign of fire. "Bah!" he sneered, "do you send all your heat to your fruit, foolish wood?" and he threw the crab apple aside.

Then he took the pine and the oak and twirled them together. In a short time a tiny flame burst forth, and soon Coyote had a big fire blazing right in front of Mosquito's door.

Mosquito spread out his hands to warm himself and shut his eyes in enjoyment. Coyote threw an armful of rotten wood on the fire in order to smother the blaze with smoke. Then Coyote turned the smoke drift into Mosquito's face. Mosquito could not catch his breath and lay down on the ground.

Coyote jumped on his head and cried: "You shall not kill any more. You have been a terror to everybody, but now your power is gone. I am going to split your head open. From it shall come a tiny race. They may fly about people's faces, and annoy them, and take a little blood, but never may they kill."

With one tremendous stroke of his stone knife, Coyote cleft the giant's head. Out poured myriads of tiny buzzing creatures. They still exist to-day, always near some water. They still remember their great ancestor. They buzz around trying to threaten as he did; they suck blood from every animal; and recollecting how he met his death, they flee before a smoke.

The children's attention to the story had been interrupted by the visitation of several mosquitoes.

"These are bad enough," exclaimed Antonio. "What must such a big mosquito have been like!"

"But, Klayukat, there is no water here. So why are there mosquitoes here?" asked Juanita.

"Here at your Señor Padre's house there is no water, but over the hill is there not the *lagunita?* There the mosquitoes breed, and from there they come over the hill to bother us sinful mortals. Ugh! They are sent by the devil to try our souls"; and Klayukat slapped his head with his two hands.

"Are they all afraid of smoke, Klayukat?" inquired Juanita.

"Every one of them will flee before smoke. They are all afraid of it," answered the old man.

"Then why don't we have a big fire and lots of smoke, and keep them away all the time?" asked Antonio.

"That, young Antonio, is for you to ask your Señor Padre."

"Let's go to him now," cried Juanita. "Hurry, I hear these mosquitoes singing, 'I'll suck your blood, suck, suck!' Don't you hear them, Tonio? Oh, Tonio, let's run"; and she led the race.

WHY THE SNAKES
CHANGE THEIR SKINS

ONE day as the children were passing Klayukat's shop, they saw him oiling a rattlesnake's skin.

"Oh, what a big snake!" and Juanita shuddered.

"Did you kill it? How many rattles did it have?" questioned Antonio.

"Twelve rattles. Yes, I killed it last evening over near the quarry."

"My! I'll never go near there any more"; and Juanita puckered up her face into a hundred wrinkles.

"Oh, rattlers will not hurt you!" Antonio assured her. "They always ring their rattles in time for you to get out of their way. What are you going to do with the skin, Klayukat?"

"It is to hold medicine. I shall oil it many times, and then it will always keep soft and whole. It will not crumble like the skins the snakes have cast off and you find on the ground."

43

" Do snakes cast off their skins?"

"Did you not know that, young Antonio?" queried the old Indian in surprise. "Yes, they throw off their skins when they need new ones. That is the law since the old times. Did you never hear why the rattlesnake changes its skin?"

"No. Why? Please tell us, Klayukat." Even Juanita edged nearer the snake skin.

Klayukat went on rubbing the skin, up and down, up and down, and his words kept rhythmic measure with his hands.

A long time ago an old witch went to an eagle's nest while he was away from home. She grabbed his older son by the neck and sucked his blood, every drop. She grabbed his younger son by the neck and sucked his blood, every drop. Then she flew down to earth.

When Eagle returned home, he called to his children. There was no answer. He looked in the nest. There were the two lifeless bodies. "Ah me! ah me!" he cried. "Who has done this awful deed?" He wheeled around in the air to see what creature was guilty. He saw all the animals busy with their own affairs; but down in the pine forest he caught a glimpse of the old witch hiding among the needles.

"Ah, that is the wretch!" he screamed. "I'll have her blood"; and he swooped down in the air above her.

The old witch heard him coming. She ran as the north wind through the trees and up to the top of the rocky cliffs. There a rattlesnake lay sunning himself.

"Save me!" cried the old witch. "O Rattlesnake, save me from the wrath of Eagle."

Rattlesnake had opened his lips to say that he could do nothing, when lo! she ran right into his open mouth.

Now Rattlesnake liked to eat all kinds of young and tender creatures; but when it came to old witches, he refused to have them in his body.

"Get out of me!" he exclaimed. "Get out of me, or I'll pitch you down the steepest precipice."

The old witch answered never a word.

"Fly out of me, or I'll swallow an eagle to battle with you"; and Rattlesnake hissed and threatened and shook his rattles to frighten her.

But the old witch never stirred.

Rattlesnake sputtered and hissed, twisted and writhed, until at last he wriggled out of his skin and left the old witch in it. He was so surprised to be rid of her that he exclaimed, "Old Witch, where are you?"

Then the old witch in the skin mocked his tone of voice and said, just as he had said, "Old Witch, where are you?"

Ever since that time snakes have shed their skins. And since then witches have lived in these old cast-off snake skins, and if you talk near one of them, an old witch will mock your words and voice.

———

"Did you ever talk near an old snake skin, Klayukat? And did a witch mock you?" Juanita's tones were awed.

"Let's try with this skin. There was no mocking when you told the story," said Antonio.

"Oh, but this skin was not cast off by the snake. I peeled this off myself. What you want is to find an old skin on the hillside, and then you will see. You will hear, too." Klayukat's voice seemed to come from the soles of his feet, so deep was it.

"Let's go to mamma, Tonio"; and Juanita slipped her hand into her brother's.

"Yes, dinner must be nearly ready now. Good morning, Klayukat. Thank you for the story."

"Good morning, children. God keep you safe until we meet again."

WHY THERE IS ONLY ONE
SOUTHWEST WIND

ONE afternoon the southwest wind was careering over the ranch, breaking trees, harassing cattle, and making things generally uncomfortable. Antonio and Juanita could not take their ride, and their book and music lessons were over. Tecla was cross and would not speak to them. She had neuralgia and went around with her head tied up in cascara leaves. After a while the children wandered over to the saddler's shop, where they found the door closed. They heard a low crooning inside. They knocked and received a welcoming "Come in, children."

"How do you like to have the wind blow this way, Klayukat?" asked Antonio, as Juanita arranged her mantilla over her head.

"Oh, very well, children, very well. The adobe is solid and the door shuts close. I remember that once there were five southwest winds, and I am glad that now there is but one. Who can tell if the roof could withstand five such winds as this?"

"Were there once five southwest winds, Klayukat? What became of the others?" and Antonio leaned against the old man's knee.

"Is there only one wind making all this noise?" shivered Juanita.

"Only one southwest wind, *Nınita*. If there were five now, you could not walk over to old Klayukat's shop, *Chiquita*. Would you like to hear why there is only one southwest wind now?"

The children's enthusiastic answers were all the inspiration old Klayukat needed. He waxed his thread and started into the story.

———

In the early days of the earth there were five southwest winds. They were very active fellows, and so there was seldom an hour when one of them was not bustling around the world. The animals were storm tossed so much that their sides were all bruised. They complained often and bitterly, but the southwest winds only roared louder and knocked them about more frequently.

One day Blue Jay said: "Let us make war on these southwest winds. Something must be done, or they will blow us to death. We might as well die fighting them."

"But how shall we reach them?" asked the other animals. "They slip off to the sky when we try to grasp them."

"That will be easy," answered Blue Jay. "We will go up to heaven to them. Let all the birds sing their sweetest songs. Then the sky will bend its ear to listen, and we will fasten it to the earth and climb up on it."

The birds began to sing, — Wren, Robin, Lark, Thrush, and all the others. They poured forth so blithe a chorus that the sky leaned down to listen. Then Nightingale burst into a silencing solo, and the sky dipped down so low that its edge touched the earth. The animals hastened to tie it to the earth with a rope of reeds. Then they scrambled up on it and climbed up, up, up, until they came near the home of the southwest winds. There they paused to plan their attack.

Blue Jay suddenly called out: "Skate, you would better go back to earth. You are so broad that you will surely be hit with an arrow."

"Do you think I am a coward?" retorted Skate. "I'm not afraid of the winds, nor of you either, you bragging Blue Jay. Come out now, boaster, and I'll fight you a duel"; and Skate raised his bow.

"I'll soon settle you," returned Blue Jay, and he shot an arrow. Skate turned his narrow side and Blue Jay's arrow flew past him to the earth. Then Skate shot an arrow. As Blue Jay saw it coming, he jumped, but he did not rise quite high enough. The arrow struck his foot, and to this day he is not a swift runner.

"Stop your quarreling, you foolish things," called the other animals. "Come and plan how to fight the southwest winds. We are so cold out here that if we do not do something soon, we shall freeze to death."

"I'll see if I can get a brand for a camp fire," said Beaver; and he started out towards the home of the southwest winds. He was creeping along the ditch behind their house, when they saw him. Before he could escape, they rushed out and caught him. After they had killed Beaver, they took him into the house and laid him in front of the fire to singe. When Beaver felt the warmth, he came to life again and crept out of the door with some of the fire hidden under his fur. Then he raced to the animals' camp and made them a fire.

As they were warming their toes, they said: "Some one must find a hole in the house of the southwest winds. You go, Skunk, and find us a hole that we can crawl through."

"Skunk ran straight down to the earth, without telling
the other animals"

"All right," answered Skunk; and he crept away. When he reached the yard of the southwest winds, they saw him. One said: "There is Skunk. He has no right to be here. Let us catch him and kill him."

Skunk heard the words. He was so frightened that he turned and fled. He ran straight down to the earth, without telling the other animals that he was going.

The animals became tired of waiting for Skunk. After a time they said, "O Robin, you go find us a hole in the house of the southwest winds, — a hole that we can crawl through."

"All right," answered Robin; and she hopped away. She found a little hole near the chimney corner and crept inside to see what the house was like. It was very warm and comfortable there. The southwest winds were sleeping, so she sat down by the fire to warm her breast and forgot to go back to her waiting brothers.

After a time the animals again wearied of waiting. They cried, "O Mouse and Rat, you two go and find a hole in the house of the southwest winds, — one that we can crawl through."

"Very well," answered Mouse and Rat; and they started off. They found the little hole by the chimney corner, and crept inside as Robin had done. The southwest winds were still sleeping. Mouse and Rat stole over to the aprons of the winds and gnawed off their bands. They crawled up the walls to the bows of the southwest winds and gnawed the strings in two. Then they stole out again and called the other animals to the hole.

The animals came pouring in with a rush. The southwest winds woke up and stretched out their hands for their aprons. They tried to tie them on, but the bands were gone. Then they reached up for their bows and tried to shoot, but the cords were cut. While they paused in surprise, the animals grappled with them.

Eagle seized one, Owl a second, Loon a third, Turkey a fourth, and Chicken Hawk the fifth. All the other animals joined around the outside, and each shot an arrow into a wind whenever he got a chance. The southwest wind in the Eagle's grasp was soon killed, and so were all the others excepting the one with whom Chicken Hawk wrestled. This fifth wind struggled desperately and finally slipped out of Chicken Hawk's grasp. Then with a loud noise he rushed out the door and across the sky.

The animals pursued him until Blue Jay called out: "We'd better turn back to earth. The wind might come back this way and cut the sky loose."

The animals turned at once and began sliding down the sky to the earth. Blue Jay could not go very fast because of his lame foot, and a number of animals got ahead of him. This made him so angry that when he reached the earth he cut the reed rope, and the sky flew up again before all the animals were down. Those that were left in the sky changed into stars. That is why to-day we see the Great Bear, and the Dog Star, and all the other animal stars.

The animals never caught the fifth southwest wind. Even to-day he wanders bustling around the world. But he has to rest sometimes, and so the animals get more peace than when his four brothers were alive to help blow them about.

———

"Did n't the other animals do anything to Blue Jay for cutting the reed rope so soon?" inquired Juanita.

"I never heard that they did. It is well that the rope was cut, for now we have the Great Bear to look at on dark nights."

"Yes; but perhaps those animals don't like to live in the sky. Perhaps —"

But Antonio interrupted with: "I wish they 'd had a stronger bird to fight with the fifth southwest wind. Why did n't they take a buzzard? I think —"

"There is the dinner call. *I* think you must tackle this southwest wind yourself, young Antonio"; and Klayukat "shooed" them out of his shop and limped over to the kitchen.

THE FOX AND
THE COYOTE

ONE evening the children were watching the full moon glide up into the sky and were discussing whether or not it was made of green cheese.

"The coyote once got into trouble by thinking that the moon was cheese," said Tecla, in her slow, round tones.

"How was that, Tecla?"

"Yes, Tecla, please tell us. Now is just the time for a story"; and Juanita buried her head in Tecla's lap.

"Well, you have been good children to-day, so I will tell it. Sit down on the floor, Nita. You are too big a girl to need holding."

"O Tecla!" and Juanita only snuggled closer.

"Well, keep still then. Don't wriggle, and I will tell you the story as my godfather told it to me."

One night the fox was standing near a pond, looking at the moon's reflection in the water.

The coyote came up and said, "Now I am going to eat you."

The fox said: "Oh, don't eat me now, Brother Coyote. There is a big piece of cheese in this pond. Help me drink up all the water, and then we will share the cheese."

The coyote looked at the reflection of the moon in the water and said: "That is a fine piece of cheese. I will help you get it."

So he drank until he felt tired, and still the pond seemed full. "Oh, Brother Fox, my stomach aches. I can't drink any more."

"Well, you stay here, and I will run and get some friends to help us drink up the water."

And away the fox ran, and although the coyote waited for him all night, he never came back.

"Poor Coyote!" murmured Juanita.

"I don't believe Coyote thought the moon was cheese," asserted Antonio. "He 'd know the difference. Wantasson says Coyote made the moon."

"Yes, perhaps Wantasson does say so; but you ask your Señora Madre who made the moon. You children don't want to believe everything that these Digger Indians tell you. Now Juanita grows heavy, and your Señora Madre calls. It is time for prayers."

"Yes, Señora, we come"; and Tecla's voice glided up the scale as she led the children in.

THE FROG IN THE MOON

THE next morning Antonio said: "I'm going to ask Klayukat about the moon and cheese. Perhaps he can tell us the truth. Come; let's go now."

They found Klayukat repairing a saddle. "Is the moon made of green cheese?" he repeated slowly. "I never heard it. I never heard of cheese in my country. You white people have many things that my tribe know nothing about. You do not see the same as we do, either."

"Don't see as you do? Why, we see with our eyes, just as you do"; and Antonio's big black eyes opened wide.

"Yes, you see with your eyes, but things do not look the same to you as they do to us. Now I have heard the white people say that there is a man in the moon, while I can see, as plainly as I see this saddle here, that there is a frog in the moon."

"A frog in the moon?" the children's voices chimed.

"Yes, a frog in the moon. I see it plainly. Besides, my people know the story of how the frog got in the moon."

Klayukat threaded his needle slowly. He started his line of stitches carefully, and then as he sewed he told this story.

In the days of the ancients the frog was very proud of his voice. He practiced singing all day and sometimes all night. When he heard a bird's song, he tried to sing the same notes.

Most of the birds just laughed at his attempts. They would call out, "Good there, Brother Frog! Now try this." Then they would sing higher, and trill and twist their notes in a sweet confusion.

Poor old Frog would try to follow their songs. He would stand on his tiptoes, but with all his trying he never could make musical sounds. Still he never was discouraged. He kept on singing day and night.

Now Whip-poor-will was not always good-natured. She liked to be alone, and she did not care to hear others sing. She thought that no one understood music as she did.

One night, after the other animals were asleep, she stole out alone into the dusk and began singing a soft tale of her sorrows. Suddenly, from the spring's bank she heard a grating voice trying to imitate her song. She listened. The voice was hushed. She sang a few more notes, and again the voice tried to repeat them. She flew in anger down to the spring. There sat little green Frog in his shining white vest.

"So it's you, you twanging Frog, is it?" demanded Whip-poor-will. "Well, if you like night singing so much, you can serve as a light for me to see by." And she seized him by one foot and threw him into the sky. There he fell with his legs all spread out and his shining white vest turned toward the earth. There you may see him yet, still furnishing light for Whip-poor-will to see by.

———

"Oh, the poor frog!" sympathized Juanita. "The birds up north seem so —"

"What kind of a bird is the whip-poor-will, Klayukat?" interrupted Antonio, seeing the old man look offended. "Does it sing like our lark?"

"I do not know, young Antonio. You must not expect an Indian to know things."

"Oh, but you do know things," insisted both children. "You know beautiful stories."

"I was only thinking about the blue jay's cutting the rope, and now this whip-poor-will," explained

Juanita. "But I suppose at other times these birds are good."

"Just like children, Juanita. Sometimes children obey their parents, and sometimes they wade in the creek."

Juanita hung her head at this reminder. Then she raised it and laughed. "Well, the blue jay's a pretty color anyway."

"Yes, a pretty color. But I can tell you why he is not prettier. No, not now," as the children looked expectant. "You have not done your morning lessons yet. That Tecla will be coming here for you. Run away now and come another time."

HOW THE ANIMALS GOT
THEIR COLORS

THAT same day, after their siesta, Antonio and Juanita tripped to the saddlery. Klayukat had just awakened. He did not answer their questions for a while, but busied himself with his work. When he seemed to be sewing regularly, Antonio ventured, "Klayukat, will you tell us now why the blue jay is not prettier?"

"The blue jay? Yes, and I can tell you why other things are not prettier. Give Ninita more room there, young Antonio, and I will tell you the story."

In the days of the ancients the animals were all the color of the earth. They knew nothing about red, white, or blue, or any other tint but dirt color, and so they were content with their clothes.

Once as they glanced out over the water, they saw a great big thing shining in the sun. They all stopped to look at it. If they watched it from one point, it looked blue. If they walked down the beach, it shone green. If they walked up the sands, it glowed rosy. Whenever they looked at it from a different position, they saw some new hue.

"What lovely thing is this?" they cried. "Let us get a nearer view of it."

They launched their canoes and rowed towards it, but ever it seemed to move just as they did, and they never came nearer to it. As the sun sank in the water, they said: "We must go home now. The lovely thing can meet the darkness alone." As they turned, the great shining thing followed them. It always kept the same distance behind them.

They were frightened. Then Blue Jay said: "Let us shoot it to-morrow. Then we can have its colors." The other animals agreed, and they all went to their homes to sleep.

As the sun brought back light to the world, the animals saw the great thing throwing out its beautiful colors. They hurried for their bows and began aiming at it. They shot all day, but their arrows always fell short of the thing, or to the left of it, or to the right. No one could hit it.

Now Blue Jay's two daughters were not on the shore. They had been sent into the woods to dig potentilla roots. While they were digging, the younger said to the older, "I wish we could shoot at the great shining thing." The elder sister went on digging with never a word in answer. After a little while the younger sister said again, "I wish we could shoot at the great shining thing." Again the elder sister went on digging without answering a word. The younger sister repeated her wish a third time and a fourth, and yet the elder sister went on digging in silence.

When for the fifth time the younger sister had said, "I wish we could shoot at the great shining thing," the elder sister stood up straight and replied, "Well, our father has arrows." Then she gathered her potentilla roots into her basket and started home. The younger sister gathered her roots into her basket and followed.

When they reached home at sunset, the animals were all sad at not having shot the great shining thing.

The next morning the daughters of Blue Jay started for potentilla roots before their father was awake. They carried off quietly two of his bows and some arrows. In the woods they hid their baskets and dressed themselves as strange youths.

When the other animals awakened, they went down to the beach to shoot at the shining thing. Again their arrows fell short of it, or to the right, or to the left. Suddenly among them appeared two strange youths. The elder shot an arrow. It fell near, but did not hit the great shining thing. Then the younger shot, and her arrow almost touched the mass of bright color. They each shot two more arrows. Some flew so near the thing that the animals held their breath, but each arrow fell a little short. Then the strange youths disappeared suddenly in the woods.

That night, when the daughters of Blue Jay carried home their baskets of potentilla roots, they found all the animals wondering who the strange youths were. Only Blue Jay was silent. He looked hard at his daughters, but they said nothing.

The next day, while the animals were shooting, the strange youths suddenly appeared again. They each shot three arrows. All flew nearer the great shining thing than the arrows of the other animals, but none touched it. Then the youths disappeared as suddenly as they had come.

The animals were greatly excited and wondered who the strange youths were. That night they told the daughters of Blue Jay about it, but the daughters were silent. Blue Jay, too, was silent, and he looked hard at his daughters.

On the third day the strange youths appeared as before. The elder shot three arrows. The younger shot two that almost reached the thing. Her third arrow pierced the middle of the splendor. Then the two youths jumped into a canoe and rowed out to the thing. They dragged it to the shore and carried it into the woods. The animals were almost crazed with excitement. "Who are these strange youths?" they asked each other. "Where did they carry the great shining thing? Why did they not give us some of it?" That night they told the sisters the story, but the sisters were silent.

The next morning the daughters of Blue Jay awoke early and went to take their bath. While they were gone, their father awoke. He looked at his daughters' bed. It was empty. He became very angry. "Where have those daughters gone now?" he stormed aloud. "I believe they are the strange youths. I shall have to punish them."

Just then the daughters came in. "Where have you been?" Blue Jay demanded. "Why do you go out so early every morning? I believe you are the two strange youths. Tell me, have you the great shining thing hidden from our people?"

"Go, take your bath, father, and then we will tell you all about it," the daughters answered.

The father took his morning dip, and then the daughters told him the whole story. "Go, bring the shining thing here," he said, "and I will call the people."

When Blue Jay had assembled all the people, the daughters came in from the woods, carrying the great shining thing. They took a knife and cut it into pieces. They handed one piece to each animal. The animals ate the pieces they received. The largest of all they gave to their father. Blue Jay was much pleased. He held it up to the light before swallowing it. But just as he was about to put it into his mouth, Clam jumped up, snatched it from him, and ran down to the beach.

Blue Jay tried to catch him, but Clam hid himself in the sand. Blue Jay took a stick and poked in the sand. Clam sent up some boiling water and hid himself deeper. Blue Jay became very angry. "You thief," he cried, "you shall hide in the sand all the days of your life. Even when your most ardent lover wishes to see you, you will send up bubbles to greet him, instead of words."

And to this day Clam lives in the sand, and he still sends up bubbles to the surface. But he has on his shell all the colors of the great shining thing, because he ate the largest piece. Blue Jay had only a little piece to eat, and so he has only blue. Every animal became in color like the piece of the great shining thing that he ate, and he has that same color even to-day.

"Oh-oh!" sighed Juanita in content. "Is the clam shell in your country like the abalone shell here, Klayukat?"

"Much the same; much the same; the same bright colors."

"I wonder what the great shining thing was made of," said Antonio. "Do you know, Klayukat?"

"Made of colors. That is why the animals changed colors when they ate it. Yesterday I saw some colors on the top of the little pond near the corral."

"Colors on our pond? Oh, let's go and see them, Nita": and the children were off on a run.

THE RACCOON AND THE
MAN-OF-TAR

ONE day Antonio was complaining because he could not catch a squirrel in his trap, when Tecla remarked: "Traps are not any good, except to catch silly birds. Animals have too much sense to go into them. You know the old Señora would never have caught the raccoon, if she had depended upon traps."

"Did a Señora catch a raccoon?" and Antonio was all interest. "How did she catch it, if she didn't use a trap?"

"This is what my godfather told me about it." Tecla sat down on a bench, and the two children leaned against her as she recited the tale.

———

Once an old lady lived in the country and had a very pretty garden. One night a raccoon came and helped himself to her watermelons and corn.

In the morning the old lady said: "Some rascally animal has been at my garden. I must set a trap to catch him."

The next night the raccoon came again, and he saw the trap. "Ah!" cried he, "here is a trap set for me. But I will play a trick on them. I will jump over it." So he jumped over it and ate all the corn and watermelons he wanted.

When the old lady found the trap untouched and her corn and melons gone, she said, "I will set traps all around the garden."

But the raccoon was not afraid of any of the traps. He jumped over them all as easily as could be and had as much supper as he could eat.

The next morning the old lady said, "Well, if I cannot catch the rascal in a trap, I will some other way." So she made a man-of-tar and put it in the garden.

That night the raccoon looked around for the traps, but there were none to be seen. "Why," he said, "they must be tired of trying to catch me."

Then he saw the man-of-tar and said: "What is this? Oh, how do you do, gentleman?"

The man-of-tar did not answer.

"Why don't you speak to me? Don't you think I am good enough to speak to a gentleman like you?"

"That night the raccoon looked around for the traps"

The raccoon waited for a reply, but the man-of-tar said never a word.

"If you don't say, 'How do you do' to me, I shall hit you"; and he raised his right fist.

Still nothing but silence followed his words.

Then the raccoon gave a hard hit, and his fist stuck fast in the tar.

"Let go! Let go, or I'll hit you with the other."

The strange dark man did not speak, neither did he let the prisoner loose.

So the raccoon struck with his left fist, and it stuck fast in the tar.

The raccoon became very angry, and his voice was loud. "If you don't let me go, I'll kick you."

The man-of-tar did not answer.

The raccoon kicked out his right foot, and it stuck fast in the tar.

"Let me go home, I say, or I'll kick you hard with my other foot."

The man-of-tar took no notice of this threat, neither by word nor by action.

The raccoon kicked out with the left foot, and it stuck fast in the tar.

"Well, I'd better not butt you," he said, "or you might hold my head fast and I could not call for help."

He called and called, but no one came to help him.

In the morning the old lady found him. She tied a rope around him, hung him to a branch of a tree, and called her cats to come and eat him. The cats were afraid and would not touch him, so she called her dog, and it came and ate the raccoon.

"She ought to have eaten it herself," said Antonio. "Wantasson says raccoons are good eating. Say, Nita, you let me take your doll to make a man-of-tar, and if I catch two squirrels, I'll give you one."

"My doll! My doll that the Good Kings put in my shoe! Why, Antonio Guerrero, I'll — "

Juanita was on the verge of tears of indignation, when Antonio shrugged his shoulders and replied: "Oh! keep your old doll. Two sticks will do as well."

Now I must explain to Joe and Mabel what Juanita meant when she said, "My doll that the Good Kings put in my shoe." The Spanish-Californian children did not hang up their stockings the night before Christmas as you do, nor did they have a Christmas tree as Dorothy does. They did not even receive any presents on Christmas. That day to them was *La Fiesta del Señor*, the "Feast of the Master"; and they spent it in rejoicing that Christ had given himself as a gift to the world. But during the Christmastide there came a day when they did receive presents.   This was on Little Christmas, the "Feast of the Epiphany," or January the sixth.   This feast, you know, is held in honor of the day on which the Three Wise Kings brought their gifts to the Infant Jesus in Bethlehem.

The evening before Little Christmas the Californian children placed their shoes outside the door or window, and the Three Wise Kings always left something in them.   It was not very much that the Kings left — just some funny little twirled candies with caraway seeds in them and some odd wooden toys.   Juanita's doll would not seem pretty to you to-day, Mabel, but she loved it just as dearly as you do your Arabella from Paris, and she was just as horrified at the idea of turning it into a man-of-tar as you were when Joe wanted to throw Arabella into the pond to teach Ponto to swim for her.

OLD DEER AND OLD GRIZZLY

ONE day the ranch was excited over a fine deer that a herder had brought in. In the late afternoon the children visited the blacksmith shop.

In talking over the way deer lose their lives, Wantasson said, "It has always been that way ever since the day Old Grizzly killed Old Deer."

"When was that, Wantasson? Won't you tell us about it?"

Never reluctant to rest, Wantasson sat down in the doorway and began the story.

In the days of the ancients Old Deer and Old Grizzly were good friends and lived together in one lodge. They each had two children. Every morning they took their baskets and went out together to dig roots.

Before leaving home Old Grizzly always said to her cubs, "Do not skip down from the house, or your hearts will get loose in you. Do not jump over logs, or tree sticks will run into you. Do not dive into the water, or it will rise and smother you."

The cubs always answered, "We will obey our mother's orders."

Old Deer never warned her children of anything. She just said, "Good-by, children."

One morning, while they were gathering roots, Old Deer filled her basket first. Old Grizzly had been eating as she dug. Old Deer said, "I'm ready to go home now"; and started on. Old Grizzly grumbled, but she went home with Old Deer, and they each gave their roots to their children.

The next morning Old Grizzly again ate the roots, instead of putting them into her basket. Old Deer worked steadily and soon had her basket full. When she started to go home, Old Grizzly in jealous anger sprang upon her neck and killed her. She hung Old Deer's body in a tree. Then she put into her own basket the roots Old Deer had gathered and returned home.

When she reached the lodge, she gave some roots to her own cubs and some to Old Deer's children. As the younger Deer child smelled the roots, he cried, "That smells like our mother."

But the older Deer child nudged him and whispered, "Be silent. Don't say that."

They put away the roots and lay awake all night watching for their mother.

In the morning Old Grizzly said to the young deer: "I must go and search for your mother. I don't see why she has not come back. She must have made a fire in the woods and have fallen asleep there." Then after telling her own children what they must not do while she was away, she set out into the woods.

When she was out of sight, the young deer said to the cubs, "Shall we play skipping down from the house?"

"Oh, no," the cubs answered, "our mother told us not to skip down from the house. It will make our hearts loose in us."

Then the young deer said, "Let's jump over logs."

"Oh, no," the cubs answered, "our mother made us promise not to jump over logs, for the tree sticks will run into our legs."

"If you will not jump," said the young deer, "let's play plunging into the water."

"Oh, no," answered the cubs, "our mother told us not to dive into the water. It will rise up and smother us."

"Well, then," said the young deer, "let's play 'Smoke Out.'"

"Our mother has not told us about that. By and by we will play it."

The young deer put rotten wood on the lodge fire. Then they said to the cubs: "We will go into the lodge. You must put the cover on, and when we call out, take it off."

"All right," said the cubs, "go in."

The young deer went in, and the cubs covered the smoke hole. After a while the deer called out,

> "Two smoke in,
> Two smoke out,
> Two smoke in,
> Smother, smother, oh, oh."

The cubs uncovered the smoke hole, and the deer came out.

Then the cubs went into the lodge, and the deer covered the hole. In a short time the cubs cried,

> "Smoke in,
> Smother, smother."

The deer uncovered the hole, and the cubs came out. After the deer had been in a second time, it was the cubs' turn again.

They went in, and the deer again covered the hole. When the cubs called,

> " Two smoke in,
> Two smoke in,
> Smother, smother,"

the deer sat on the cover and would not let them out.

When the cubs were smothered to death, the young deer drew them up. They took some red paint, which Old Grizzly had stolen from the Indians, and lined the cubs' faces. The older one they propped up on the top of the lodge, with a stick under his mouth to keep it closed. The younger cub they tied to the ladder and put a stick under his mouth to keep it closed.

Then they went into the lodge and said to the fireplace: " Fireplace, do not tell Old Grizzly which way we have gone. She killed our mother and so we have killed her children." The fireplace promised that it would not tell. And so they bound everything in the lodge not to tell, everything but the bone awl. They did not notice this because it was sticking in the ceiling. Then they started away.

When Old Grizzly approached her home again, she saw her cubs on the roof and ladder. She noticed the red paint on their faces. She became angry. "I'll punish you well for wasting my red paint," she cried. "I'll teach you not to play with such things."

As she came nearer, she saw that her children were dead. She dropped her basket and wailed, "Oh! the children of Old Deer have punished me."

Then she cried, "Oh, children, where are you?"

She went into the lodge and asked, "Fireplace, which way did Old Deer's children go?" The fireplace was silent.

She questioned each article in the lodge, but received no answer until she came to the bone awl. It said, "The children of Old Deer went to the east."

Old Grizzly started after them. As the evening star climbed up the sky, she came to a cave blockaded with stones. She knew the young deer were in it. She called out loud: "To-morrow when it is light, I shall play a game with you children. Then I shall be able to see."

The older child was awakened. It shook the younger and whispered: "She has overtaken us. We must plan what to do."

They watched Old Grizzly build a fire and lie down beside it. After a while she snored. The deer children threw little sticks near her. She did not stir. They threw larger sticks. She did not stir. They threw small stones and large stones.

Still she did not stir. Then they stole out of the cave and ran away through the woods.

When they came to the river, they called out to Old Crane: "Cross us over very fast, O Uncle, else Old Grizzly will overtake us."

Old Crane hurried across to them. They told him the story of Old Grizzly's killing their mother, and of their revenge and flight. Old Crane was very fond of Old Deer, so he lifted up his voice and wailed, "*É-ush tchiwa, é-ush tchiwa.*"

Crane's children also wept aloud, "*É-ush tchî tchû tchî tchû.*"

Then Old Crane crossed them over the river and blew upon them. They stiffened out upon the ground and looked like two whistle sticks.

When Old Grizzly was awakened by the morning star, she growled, "Now, at last, I shall play a game with you children." She rushed to the cave. The children were gone. She followed their tracks to the river. There she hallooed to Old Crane, "Come and cross me over the river."

Old Crane came slowly.

"Hurry, Old Crane. I want to overtake Old Deer's children. Have you seen them? Are they on your side of the river."

"There are no deer children on my side," answered Old Crane.

"You are deceiving me," growled Old Grizzly. "You are trying to conceal them. Here are their tracks. Now cross me over fast."

"I have no canoe," objected Old Crane.

"You need no canoe. Cross me over fast," insisted Old Grizzly.

Old Crane spread out his legs across the river, making a bridge from one side to the other. Old Grizzly stepped on his legs and began walking over. When she was halfway across, she felt thirsty. She seized Old Crane's skullcap and drank from the river. Then, to empty the cap, she gave it a hit against Old Crane's leg. This angered Old Crane. He drew down his leg and doused Old Grizzly in the river.

Then he blew upon the whistle sticks, and they turned into Old Deer's children. They took the bows of Old Crane's children and shot Old Grizzly dead.

———

While Wantasson had been telling his story, Klayukat had come to the shop, his punch in his hand. When the story was finished, he said, "A very good tale that, Wantasson. My people have one something like it, only it is of the robin and the salmon berry, and it goes farther and tells how the trees got their uses."

"Oh, tell that story to us, Klayukat. Oh, please!" cried the children.

"Not now, little ones. You have had your story and a good one, too. Now Wantasson will fix my punch for me, and you go to your play."

THE ROBIN AND THE
SALMON BERRY

EVIDENTLY Klayukat expected the children the next morning, for he had a basket of hazelnuts cracked for them. "You eat these," he said, "and while I stitch, I will tell you the story we spoke of."

"But first, Klayukat, what is a salmon berry?" asked Antonio. "Has it anything to do with a salmon?"

"Nothing to do with a salmon except its color. It is salmon colored when it is ripe. It is a berry that is something like your blackberry, only it is not black, and it does not grow on a vine. It grows on a bush."

"Oh!"

The children began crunching the nuts, and Klayukat began his tale.

Robin and Salmon Berry were sisters. They lived in different parts of the same house. Robin had five children, and they were all girls. Salmon Berry had five children, and they were all boys.

Every day Robin and Salmon Berry went picking berries together. One evening, as they walked toward home, Salmon Berry noticed that Robin's berries were all unripe, for Robin had eaten the ripe ones as she found them. Her own basket was filled with luscious berries. Robin looked at Salmon Berry and said, "What would you think if I should eat you?"

Salmon Berry replied, "Don't do that. My children would be poor without me."

That night Salmon Berry told her children: "That monster said she would like to eat me. If she really should eat me, don't stay here any longer, else she will eat you also. If she tries to deceive you, do not believe her."

One night Robin came home alone. "Your mother lost her way," she said to the Salmon Berry children.

"Behold, she has killed her," thought the eldest son of Salmon Berry.

He stayed awake all night for fear that Robin would eat him and his brothers while they were sleeping.

In the morning Robin said: "I will search for your mother. She must be lost in the woods."

When she was out of sight, Salmon Berry's eldest son made a fire. He said to Robin's children: "Let's play a game. Let's steam each other. You steam us first, and then we will steam you. When we cry, ' Now we are done,' you must let us out of the hole."

"All right," said the children of Robin.

They heated stones and put them in the hole. Then Salmon Berry's children went into the hole. Robin's children piled dirt up over them. After a while the eldest son called out, "Now we are done," and Robin's children uncovered them and let them out.

They heated stones again and put them into the hole. Robin's children went in. The children of Salmon Berry covered them up with dirt and piled heavy sticks on top of them. Soon Robin's children called, "We are done"; but the children of Salmon Berry would not let them out. Robin's children cried a little while and then were silent. They were dead. All five were dead.

The children of Salmon Berry took them out of the hole. They put one near a pond of water and twisted its mouth so that it looked as if it were laughing. They put another in the water of the pond. This was the youngest robin child. Still another they put on the roof where it seemed to be looking for its mother. The fourth they stood upright near the door of the house, while they placed the fifth on the sand so that it looked as if it were playing with shells. Then they dug a hole. They left their dog at the mouth of the hole and they escaped through it.

Robin came home at night. She thought to herself, "Now I will eat the eldest son."

She noticed something floating on the water, but did not stop to examine it. She went straight to the house, and said to the child sitting upright near the door, "Where is your youngest sister?" The child did not answer. She pushed her, and her finger went right into her flesh.

She saw the child on the roof. "Where is your youngest sister?" she called. The child did not answer. She pulled at its arm, and the arm came out.

She went to the child playing in the sand. "Where is your youngest sister?" but the child did not answer. She put her hand on its head, and the head rolled off.

She saw the child sitting near the pond with its mouth twisted as if it were laughing. "You cruel thing!" she cried, "I cannot find your youngest sister, and you are laughing." She pulled the child's hair, and it came out.

When she saw the youngest child floating on the water, she went in to pull it out, and it came to pieces. Then she wailed, " Oh, Salmon Berry's son has killed my children."

She went to the house and looked around for her nephews. Then she noticed the dog. " Which way did your masters go?" she asked him.

"*Wu!*" answered the dog, pointing with his mouth in one direction.

Robin ran that way and tried to smell the tracks of the children of Salmon Berry. She could find no trace of them. She returned to the dog. " You are deceiving me," she accused him. " Tell me which way your masters have gone."

"*Wu!*" answered the dog, and pointed his mouth in another direction. Robin ran where he had pointed, but she could find no trace of the children of Salmon Berry. She came back to the dog and scolded him again. Five times did the dog turn her from the right track. Then she discovered the hole.

She ran down it and found the tracks of the children. She followed them, calling as she ran, " O children! I have found your mother."

The children of Salmon Berry heard her and ran faster. The youngest grew tired, and the others took turns in carrying him. After a while they came to the skins of two elk bucks. The eldest son found two kettles and boiled the skins in one and the antlers in another, and he said to each: "When Robin reaches you, you must boil violently. Don't cool off too quickly, for she will be hungry and will forget to pursue us while she waits to eat." Then the children ran on.

Robin came to the kettles. They were both boiling violently. She began to scold the kettle of skins. "I will take revenge on your grandmother, your mother, and all your relatives." The skins could not stand this. They stopped boiling. They cooled off. Robin ate, and ate, and ate, until she finished all that was in the kettle of skins.

Then she looked at the kettle of antlers and began to scold it. "I will take revenge on your father, your uncle, your mother, and all your relatives." The antlers could not stand this. They stopped boiling and cooled off. Robin ate, and ate, and ate, until she had eaten all that was in the kettle of antlers. Then she went on as quickly as she could.

Meanwhile the children of Salmon Berry had reached the creek. They saw Old Crane near the water and asked him to take them across.

"Don't be afraid, children," he answered. "Go to my house and eat there. Fish has been boiled for you." They went to Old Crane's house and ate and rested.

Robin came to the creek. She called, "Younger Brother, take me across." She called this many times. Then Old Crane came over slowly. He stretched his legs out and bridged the water. He said to Robin, "Don't be afraid, or you might fall in."

Robin started to walk across on his leg. When she was halfway over, she became frightened, for the leg there was narrow. Old Crane began to shake his leg, and he shook it so hard that Robin fell into the water. As she was floating downstream, she heard Old Crane calling after her: "Robin shall be your name, Robin shall be your name. But no more shall you eat people."

The current first swept Robin against jagged rocks, which cut her breast, and then it landed her upon a sandy beach. There she lay still and seemed to be dead. The crow came and pecked at the hole in her breast. The blood flowed out, and Robin stirred a little. "Stop eating me, Old Crow," she murmured, "I am alive." The crow flew away. Robin lay still awhile.

When the blood had stopped flowing and had caked itself over her breast, she arose and started homeward through the woods. On her way she passed a willow and said to it, "O Willow, is my painting becoming?"

The willow sighed, "Oh, how bad looks the blood on her breast!"

"Oh, you bad thing!" answered Robin. "When your wood burns, it will crackle and give out little heat."

Then she came to an alder and asked, "O Alder, is my painting becoming?"

The alder bowed quietly. "It is becoming, the blood of your breast."

"Ah, little sister," laughed Robin; "when people want color, they will get red dye from your bark. When you are dry, you will burn with a steady heat."

She next came to a cottonwood. "O Cottonwood, is my painting becoming?"

"Oh, how bad looks the blood of her breast!" murmured the cottonwood.

"Oh, you horrid thing! You shall have breaks in your side, and you will not burn well when you are dry."

Then she passed to the maple and asked, "O Maple, is my painting becoming?"

"Oh, how becoming is the blood of her breast!" nodded the maple.

"Ah, you are true, dear sister. Your bark shall be used for baskets, and people shall find them of great use."

When she came to the vine maple, she asked as before, "Is my painting becoming?"

"Oh, how becoming is the blood of her breast!" replied the vine maple.

"You answer well, and your wood shall be used for dishes and spoons, and for all things to make a house comfortable."

Then she passed to the cedar and asked, "O Cedar, is my painting becoming?"

"Oh, how becoming is the blood of her breast!" answered the cedar.

"You speak well, my younger brother. When people make canoes of you, they will be able to exchange them for slaves. They shall use you for houses and sell these for values."

Then she went to the fir and asked, "O Fir, is my painting becoming?"

"Oh, how becoming is the blood of her breast!" sighed the fir.

"You are wise, O Fir. When conjurers chant their songs, your wood shall be burned in their sacred fires. Your breath shall ever be sought after by people. You will always be a healer of woes."

Thus Robin passed through the forest, giving to each tree the uses that it has to-day.

"And did that horrid robin give every tree its use — every single tree?" inquired Juanita.

"Every tree that has a use got it from Robin that day."

"And was the hazel tree told to raise these nuts?" and Antonio held up the few that were left in the basket.

"It was told that day."

"Well, they're good nuts, but I wish that old Robin hadn't told them to grow," said Juanita, as she stood up and shook her skirt in disdain.

"You may have more nuts some other day. Now go to the house before that Tecla comes calling for you."

HOW THE ANIMALS
SECURED SALMON

HE next day Juanita said, "When Klayukat told us about the robin and salmon berry, why did n't we ask him if he knew a story about the real salmon?"

"Let's go and ask him now, though I don't see that a salmon could do much — living always in the water."

"But the salmon berry children did much. Why not a salmon? Wilt thou ask him, Tonio?"

"Yes. Come along," and they walked across to the saddlery.

"About a salmon? Well, I know how the animals first got salmon. Will that do? Yes? Well, sit on the hides, and I will tell you that story."

In the olden times there were a great many salmon in the sea, but none could get up the river.
Five old beaver sisters built a dam at the mouth of
the river and would not let them pass.

The animals up the river were starving. They
had eaten all the berries and nuts and roots of
the past year, and there would be no more food
for them for three moons. They went in a body
to Coyote and prayed, "O Coyote! get us some
salmon, else our bones will cut through our
skins."

"I will think what to do," answered Coyote. He
thought and thought and thought. Then he made
a boat and started down alone to the mouth of the
river.

When he got near the dam, he changed himself
into an Indian baby tied to a papoose board. Then
he lay in the bottom of the boat and floated until
he was just above the dam. Just then one of the
five sisters came out to the river's edge. As soon
as Coyote saw her, he began to wail like a little
baby. She waded in and brought the canoe to
shore.

Then she called to her sisters: "O sisters! I
have found a baby. His mother must have been
drowned from the canoe, and he has floated down
alone."

"She waded in and brought the canoe to shore"

The other sisters crowded around to see him and to pinch his round little cheeks. He began to cry. Then they said, " Let us give him some food."

They gave him shredded salmon, and it tasted very good to hungry Coyote. He laughed and held up his tiny hands. They laughed with him and pinched his cheeks and caressed him. Then they took him to their camp and left him alone while they went out to watch the dam.

After they had disappeared, Coyote changed back to his own form. He hunted around for the key of the dam. He did not find it, but he found some dried salmon and ate it.

The sisters came home at sundown. They saw only the little baby on a papoose board in the corner where they had left him. When they missed their dried salmon, they exclaimed, "This is strange"; but they did not suspect the baby.

The next sunrise the sisters went to guard the dam. Coyote became himself again, and again searched for the key. He did not find it, but he found and ate some more dried salmon. At night, when the sisters missed their food, they said, "This is wonderful." They looked keenly at the baby on the papoose board in the corner. He smiled and cooed, "Goo, goo!" They smiled back and said, "No, it cannot be the baby."

This happened for four suns. On the fifth Coyote found the key to the dam hanging on a knot of an elder tree. So fast did he run to the river that the earth trembled beneath his steps.

The sisters, sitting at the dam, were shaken. "This is amazing," they said. "That baby must be a monster."

Just then they saw Coyote in his own form running towards them. They seized clubs and fell upon him. He wriggled away and plunged into the water. He swam to the door of the dam and unlocked it. The river roared through, breaking away the whole dam in its hurry. Then the salmon swam up the river, and ever since, to this day, the animals have not needed to go hungry.

"What funny old Señoras to give a baby dried salmon!" laughed Juanita. "I never knew of people's giving a baby salmon, did you, Tonio?"

"But this was not a real baby. It was Coyote, so it didn't matter what they gave him. He could eat anything. So could I now. Let's go and ask Maria for a *tortilla*." And with a "Thank you, Klayukat," both children started to the kitchen.

WHY THE TICK IS
NOW SMALL

ONCE, when Antonio was out with the herders, a wood tick got on his arm. It burrowed its head into his flesh and had to be cut out. When he returned home, Juanita was much interested in his experience. Under her sympathy Antonio felt himself a man. They walked over to the saddlery talking of it.

"Just look at Tonio's arm, Klayukat. He had a tick in it, and it had to be cut out," boasted the little sister.

"A tick? Let me see. Huh! Yes. It is well for you the tick is not so large as it was before Coyote conquered it, else you would not be here to show your arm."

The arm was forgotten. Another story? They pleaded for it at once, and soon they were seated on the hides, and Klayukat was reciting the story as he stitched on his saddlebags.

———

In the ancient days Tick was a great monster. He lived on the sheltered side of a mountain and kept large herds of deer, elk, mountain sheep, and other animals that are good for food. No matter how hungry the people in the valley might be, Tick could always satisfy himself by going out among his herds and killing a fat animal.

One parching summer Coyote was nearly starving. He thought to himself: " Tick has plenty to eat, and he does no good to the animals. I will go to his house and kill him and take his herds."

He toiled up the mountain and found Tick just out of the sweat-house and ready for a plunge into the lake.

" Good morning," said Coyote. " I am tired and dusty. May I have a sweat and a bath to refresh me for the rest of my journey ? "

" You may," replied Tick, " if you will heat the rocks yourself. I have to take my bath."

" Thank you ; that I will do," answered Coyote, as he began to pile the stones on the smoldering fire. When the rocks were heated, he placed them in the sweat-house. Then he went in and closed the door tight.

"What a strange sweat-house this is!" he re-marked to himself. "It looks like the body of a big deer." And that is just what it was.

As the heat radiated from the stones, the fat on the ribs of the deer melted and dripped down. Coyote held up his mouth and caught the deli-cious drops. As his hunger was satisfied, he grew stronger, and he began to make his plans for killing Tick. When he was well sweated, he ran out of the deer house and plunged into the lake. The cool bath made him feel like a new person.

In his strength he rushed to where Tick was lying in the sun. He seized him and began to choke him. Tick lay so still that soon Coyote thought he was dead and loosened his hold.

Immediately Tick jumped up and called to all his herds to flee with him. The great deer that had formed the sweat-house shook itself and started to run to the valley. As it fled, Tick clung to its hair and was being carried away.

He laughed as he saw Coyote's look of surprise. "Aha! You thought to kill me by squeezing me. You ought to have had more sense. Why did you not put me on a rock and crush me with a stone? I'll still revel in the blood of your animals. Aha!"

The taunting laugh maddened Coyote, and he cursed Tick. "You will never more kill any of my

"He plunged into the lake"

animals. You shall be little and feeble. As you now cling to the deer's hair, so all the rest of your days you shall crawl around on the hair of animals. You shall suck blood, yes, but it will be in such tiny drops that you will never again grow fat. And at any time my animals may kill you with a stone."

So since that day Tick has been a little flat crawling creature that lives by sucking blood. The animals are no longer obedient to him, for at any time they can crush him to death by sudden violence.

———

"Oh, Tonio, I'm so glad Coyote conquered him. Just think, if the big tick had taken hold of you!" and Juanita gave her brother's arm a squeeze.

"But it didn't," said Antonio, pulling his arm loose. "Klayukat, the herders say that rabbits have ticks all over them. Is that so?"

"Who can tell? Who can tell? Ticks will go anywhere they can. As for rabbits, well, rabbits have not the best sense. Did I ever tell you the story of the jack rabbit's fight with the sun?"

"No, we've never heard it. Will you tell it to us now?"

"Not now. I must take this awl to the smithy. You come around some other time, when you have nothing to do."

WHY THE SUN TRAVELS
REGULARLY

THE next day the children appeared at Klayukat's door and asked for the rabbit story.

"We meet the rabbits everywhere we go," said Antonio, — "on the hill, in the canyon, by the road, and under our own fig trees. We'd like to know something about them."

"You may not learn much about the jack rabbit, but you will learn what a good thing he did for the world," returned Klayukat. Then, as he bored holes in some leggins, he recited this tale.

In the days of the ancients the sun did not move around the earth regularly, as it does to-day. At times it would stay away so long that all the animals would be nearly frozen. Then it would come back so close to the world that people would be burned up.

Once, when the sun had been absent a long time, Jack Rabbit sat near his camp fire with his children. They were watching for the sun to return. After a while Jack Rabbit grew weary and fell asleep.

Suddenly he was awakened. "Father, father!" he heard his children cry, "your back is on fire." Jack Rabbit rolled over in the dirt and put the fire out. He was very angry with the sun for coming back and burning him in his sleep.

"You stay here, children," he cried. "I am going to fight that sun. I am tired of its whims."

He picked up his bow and five arrows, and turned his steps toward the east.

After traveling a long while he came to the edge of the world, where the sun comes up. There he sat down and waited. After some time the sun came in sight.

"Now I shall punish you," cried Jack Rabbit, and he shot an arrow at its face. The sun only grinned and burned up the arrow before it was a mile from the earth.

Jack Rabbit sent a second arrow, but it too was burned. So was the third arrow and the fourth. The fifth arrow was a charmed one, and to make doubly sure that it would not burn, Jack Rabbit wet

it with a tear from his eye. Then he aimed carefully. Twang! The arrow flew straight to the sun
and chipped off a number of pieces from its face.

The fiery fragments came whirling down to the
earth and set everything on fire. Jack Rabbit had
to race before the flames. He jumped and jumped,
but the flames ate his toes off. He hopped faster,
but the fire caught his legs and burned them off.
He jerked on still faster, but the sparks flew on his
body and burned it up. His head bounded on still
faster. The flames reached for it. The head stumbled against a stone. Then from Jack Rabbit's eyes
poured such a flood of tears that it quenched the
fire, and the earth was saved.

Jack Rabbit crouched down under a bush near
the stone until his body and legs and toes grew
again. Then he ran back to his waiting children.

He complained to the animals about the sun's
irregularity. "It either stays away so long that we
freeze, or it comes so close that we scorch," he said.
"And if we complain, it tries to burn the whole world
up. I think we ought to order its movements."

The other animals answered, "We think so too.
Let us call a council and order the sun's movements."

So they called a council of all the animals on
the face of the earth. They sat around in a circle,

and each animal expressed his opinion. Then they all decided that the sun could not travel in such an irregular way any longer. They ruled that it should travel around the world every day, and that it should never go so far away that people would freeze, nor approach so near that they would be burned.

Ever since that council the animals have had regular days and regular seasons, and they have had no more fear of the sun's destroying them.

———

"Poor rabbit, to have his head bounce along alone," breathed Juanita. "I should think he would never have gotten well again."

"Do rabbits' tears always put out fires, Klayukat? Tecla told us that a rabbit's tear would charm an arrow," and Antonio's tones were serious.

"Did she, — that woman? So they know that in her country! Yes, a rabbit's tear will make an arrow fly straight, and if you carry some rabbit tears with you, you will never burn."

"But where do you get the tears?"

"Now that question, young Antonio — But there is that Tecla calling you. You must go," and Klayukat settled in relief to his work.

THE SUBJUGATION OF
THE THUNDERBIRD

ONE day there was a thunderstorm. At such an unusual occurrence as this, in the vicinity of San Francisco, the children were frightened. Juanita would not leave her mother's lap, and Antonio stayed close beside her. Together they said their prayers aloud. The sun was out some time before they cared to go into the courtyard. Then they sought Klayukat.

"Did you ever hear such noise before, Klayukat? Such awful noise!"

"Oh, I do not mind that noise. It cannot do any harm since Coyote made the law against it."

"Did Coyote have anything to do with thunder?"

"Yes, a great deal to do with it. If it had not been for Coyote, perhaps this thunder to-day would have killed us all."

The children clasped each other's hands.

"Sit down on the hides, and I will tell you the story."

———

In the early days Thunder was a mighty bird. He lived in the high mountains and rode about on the clouds. His only pleasure seemed to be in killing the animals. If he saw a bear taking a stroll, or an eagle soaring into the heavens, he would spread out dark clouds, pour down heavy rain, and wink his flashing eyes. He did not stop until his victim was quite dead. The animals became so frightened that they dared not step out of their houses.

One day Coyote came along and said: " What 's the matter with you people? You look frightened and hungry. Why don't you come out of your houses and hunt for food?"

"Oh, we dare not," they replied. "If we venture forth, Thunderbird pierces us with his fiery eye. Cannot you help us, O Coyote?"

"Why, this is serious," answered Coyote. "I will see what I can do."

He thought and thought and thought. Then he changed himself into a tiny downy feather and floated off on the wind. He sailed until he was over the home of Thunderbird. He looked well at the troublesome giant, then came down in a whirlwind and lighted on a dry sunflower stalk, right in front of Thunderbird's door.

Thunderbird had been watching the feather for some time. He thought, " That looks like a feather, and yet it looks like an animal." Then he sat up and took a better look at it.

" Probably," he said, " it is only a feather that I knocked out of an owl the other day. The wind has blown it here. I will try a little rain on it and see what it will do."

Then he roared in a loud tone of voice and sent down a heavy shower of rain. The feather did not move while he was doing this.

When Thunderbird ceased, the feather rose in the air and began to send down rain and thunder and most awful lightning.

Thunderbird was amazed to see such a tiny thing as a feather send down rain and thunder and lightning. " How is this?" he questioned. " I thought that *I* was the only Thunderbird in the world." Then, feeling jealous, he cried louder, winked quicker, and sent down heavier showers.

The feather replied with still fiercer thunder, keener lightning, and swifter rain, right into the very eyes of Thunderbird, and made him blink and dodge.

He was angrier than ever and returned the heaviest charges that he had. Still the feather neither blinked nor dodged, but just kept on pouring out thunder, and lightning, and rain.

Then Thunderbird flew from his rocky home into the heavens and tried to grapple with the feather. The noise was so great, and the lightning so cutting, and the rain so violent that the earth beneath was torn and burned into ravines.

Finally they came together in one close grip and fell to the earth. The shock was so great that the whole world trembled. The feather came down on top, and when it struck the earth, it turned back into Coyote.

He at once began to beat Thunderbird's head with his war club. Thunderbird pleaded for mercy, but Coyote kept on beating him until his club was shattered. Then he said: "You may live, but no more shall people see your huge body. No more may you kill or terrify. You may thunder only in the sultry summer time. You may lightning occasionally, but never more to destroy."

From that day the power of Thunderbird has been broken. He is no longer seen, and his voice and his winkings are no longer a terror to the animals.

"Oh, I'm so glad Coyote ever lived," sighed Juanita. "I'm going to pray for him to-night, the good thing, for stopping the thunder. Just think if that awful bird could swoop down on us now!"

"That is not the only awful bird Coyote conquered. There was the owl. He was nearly as bad as Thunderbird."

"The owl? I'm not afraid of an owl," and Antonio's tones betokened his bravery. "I helped Santo take one out of the barn loft."

"Huh! An owl out of a barn loft? That is not the kind Coyote dealt with. Why, it could carry off the whole barn in one claw. Owl in a barn loft — huh!" And no pleading could win another word from Klayukat that afternoon.

WHY THE BAT IS BLIND

THE children went on to the smithy. Wantasson asked, "How did you like the thunder this morning, children?"

"We didn't like it at all. Did you, Wantasson?"

"No, I did not like it, nor the lightning either. I shut the door of the shop, but the light came in so bright that I was afraid my eyes would burn out."

"We hid our eyes, didn't we, Tonio?" The brother vouchsafed no answer.

"I would have covered mine, only I had nothing here but hot iron. That would have been as bad as the pitch the bat used."

"What pitch did the bat use?" asked Juanita.

"Why did the bat use pitch?" and Antonio was all interest.

"Don't you know how the bat came to be blind? No? Well, sit down, and I will rest while we have that story."

———

Once there was no fire in this land, but the animals knew there was plenty far off in the west. One day, as they were shivering together, Bat said to Lizard, "Why don't you scurry off to the west and get a coal for us?"

Lizard said, "I believe I will." He wriggled off for many suns, until he reached the fiery west. There he took a coal in his mouth and started home.

It had not been much trouble for him to whisk unseen into the west and to take a coal, but it was not easy to get the coal safe to his home. He had to carry the brand up high, so that it would not set the grass afire; and then, too, all the animals were eager to steal fire. He had to travel at night for fear of thieves.

When he was only one sun from home, he suddenly came across a party of cranes sitting up late, gambling by the light of the moon. He crept into the shadow of a log and stole quietly on, but he could not escape their sharp eyes.

"Why, there's Lizard with a coal," screamed one crane.

"Let's get the fire. Let's get it," they all yelled, and started after him with all the speed of their long legs.

They soon overtook him, and as they snatched for the fire, Lizard dropped the coal. In a twinkling the dry grass was ablaze. Lizard speeded for his life. The burning grass followed him in great waves of flame.

Bat saw the fire approaching and rubbed her eyes to see what the matter was. Then her eyes began to pain her. She heard Lizard running in and called: "Oh, Lizard, Lizard! My eyes will be burned out with this great blaze. Please put some pitch over them to keep out the strong light."

"All right," said Lizard. He spread the pitch on, but he was trembling so that he got it on too thick. Bat could not see at all.

"Oh, now I'm blind indeed," she cried. She jumped this way and that. She fluttered against a tree and fell to the ground. Her feathers caught fire and were all singed off. She lifted herself and flew towards the west. "O, West Wind," she sobbed, "blow on my aching eyes."

The wind heard her and laid its cool fingers upon her. It could not get all the pitch off, and so Bat's eyes have always been covered since. Her feathers, too, have never grown on again, and even to this day she wears a dingy singed coat.

————

"The poor bat! How does it get around?" and Juanita looked pensive.

"It does not get around very well; it keeps bumping into things. Santo caught one in the barn last night. He had it nailed up on the barn door."

"Oh, let's go and see it"; and Antonio raced off Juanita followed, and soon they both were swinging on the lower half of the barn door, examining the bat nailed to the upper half.

Now, Mabel and Joe, I wonder if you have ever learned whether the bat is really blind. Suppose you find out about it.

WHY THE OWL EATS ONLY
SMALL CREATURES

ANTONIO and Juanita had studied the tastes of their story-tellers, and the next morning they appeared at Klayukat's door with a handful of ripe olives.

"These are for you, Klayukat. They are this year's crop and just fresh from the brine."

Klayukat extended his hand and received the dripping purple globes. As he ate, the children watched him in silence. When he had wiped his mouth on his sleeve and returned to his saddlebags, Antonio ventured, "Could you tell us this morning how Coyote conquered the owl, Klayukat?"

"I think I could." The olives had softened his mood. "Sit down and I will tell it to you."

In the days of the ancients Owl was a terror to the animal people. He was enormous in size, with great staring eyes. Every time he felt hungry, he flew down to the roadside. When an animal came along, he would jump out in front of it suddenly and demand in a loud screech: "Who are you? Who? Who?" The animal would be so frightened that it could not answer.

Then Owl would hoot: "You do not know who you are. Who? Who? I'll eat you up." And he would swallow the trembling creature. He ate so many that every family was in mourning.

The animals went to Coyote and prayed: "O Coyote, help us. This dreadful Owl is eating our brothers, our wives, and our children. Every home is filled with sobs. Oh, help us, Coyote."

"I'll see what I can do," answered Coyote.

He thought and thought. Then he brushed up his clothes and made himself look nice and young. He took his stone knife and sauntered down the road.

Suddenly Owl jumped out from the brush and demanded in his loud screech: "Who are you? Who? Who?"

Coyote looked surprised. He bowed politely and said, "Why, where did you come from?"

Then Owl looked surprised. He blinked his eyes and did not say a word.

Coyote looked straight at him and repeated, "Where did you come from?"

Owl blinked his eyes again, but he did not speak a word.

A third time Coyote asked, "Well, where did you come from?"

Owl shifted all his weight to his right foot. He blinked his eyes and said slowly in a calm voice, "Where did *you* come from?"

"I am from no other land than this where you are living," answered Coyote. "This is my country, and I am looking for something to eat."

Owl thought to himself, "I never saw this creature before. Who can he be?" Aloud he said, "I have traveled all over this country, but I never met you before."

"Why, I have been from one end of the world to the other," replied Coyote. "I have been where the sun rises and into the land of darkness. I have been up into the long colds and down into the long heats. But I never saw *you* before."

Owl blinked his eyes, but did not speak a word.

"However, I've heard of you," continued Coyote. "I've heard that you claim to have been eating people. Let's both bring the bones of the people we ate yesterday, and then we shall see which of us is the greater."

J.W.Ferguson Kennedy

" He was enormous in size, with great staring eyes "

"Yes, that is good," agreed Owl; and he went for the bones.

When Coyote heard him returning, he called in a loud tone: "Let us both shut our eyes until we get our piles fixed. Don't open them until I give the word."

"That is all right," answered Owl. He shut his eyes and went on piling the bones of the animals he had eaten.

Coyote held his eyes half open. He looked across at Owl's pile of bones. They were of large, strong animals. His own were only mice bones. He quietly drew Owl's pile before himself and put his bones before Owl. Then he called, "Let us open our eyes and see which is the greater."

They opened their eyes. Owl looked surprised at the little mice bones before him. Coyote looked at him in scorn.

"Ah, you have been deceiving us," he said. "You see you eat only mice, while I eat large animals. Therefore I am the greater."

"But I am sure I ate larger things," insisted Owl. "Let us bring the bones of our day-before-yesterday's dinner."

"That is good," answered Coyote. "And we'll shut our eyes in the same way, until I give the word to open them."

This time, too, Coyote peeped and changed around the piles of bones.

Again Owl was much surprised to see only mice bones before himself. "Let us try the day-before-the-day-before-yesterday's dinner," he said. "I am sure I have eaten larger game." Coyote consented.

They did this for five times. Each time Coyote shifted around the two piles of bones. Every time Owl was surprised to see mice bones before himself, and asked for another trial.

After the fifth time Coyote said: "You have made believe that you have been eating large animals, while you can show only mice bones. Hereafter you can eat nothing larger than mice. You've been doing enough killing. I'm going to kill you now."

Then he walked up to Owl and cut off his head with his stone knife. He took the body and threw it toward the mountains. "You may stay there, but you shall be small all the rest of your days. You may hoot, and scream, and frighten people, but nevermore may you kill them."

Since Coyote made this law, Owl has been small in size. He lives in lonely places. He often frightens people by demanding in a loud screech: "Who are you? Who? Who?" But never since that day has he been able to kill an animal larger than a mouse.

———

"I wish Coyote had n't let him eat little birds," said Juanita.

Antonio noticed a coolness returning to Klayukat's face, so he hastened with "Well, everything eats what 's smaller than itself. The birds eat bugs, and we eat the birds, so we are as bad as the owl."

"Oh, Tonio!"

"Yes, we are. We 're worse, for we eat our own chickens, and our own beef, and — and — oh, our own everything."

"Oh, Tonio! Don't; I don't want to think we are worse than the owl. I won't eat any more meat. No, don't tell me any more ' We 're worse's, for I won't hear them," and the little girl covered her ears with her hands and ran from the shop.

WHY THE DEAD DO
NOT COME BACK

ONE day Juanita was mourning the loss of a pet canary. Antonio had gone off for the day with the herders, and she was lonely in her sorrow. She went over to the saddlery to tell Klayukat her trouble.

"Just think, Klayukat, it won't sing any more. It used to love so to sing. Captain Bangs says it sang all those long days when he was bringing it from China. And now it will never sing any more," and sobs choked her words.

"Oh, *Ninita mia*, weep not so. I think your bird is singing more happily in the Land of the Dead. You know when Coyote went there he found all the dead singing and dancing and having a good time."

"Did he? When did he go? How did he go?" and Juanita's voice became firmer.

"You sit on the hides, *Chiquita*, and eat these nuts, and old Klayukat will tell you what Coyote learned about the Land of the Dead."

———

Many, many moons ago, the animal people had one sorrow, — their relatives who died never came back again. The whole land was filled with mourning, for almost every household had lost one of its number. Eagle's wife was gone, and he wept all day and would not be comforted.

Coyote felt sorry for the animals. "The leaves come back to the trees," he thought. "Why should not people come back to the earth? I ought to be able to do something to bring them back."

He went to Eagle and said: "Don't grieve so, Brother Eagle. I think people ought to come back like the leaves on the trees. Wait until spring. Then, when the grass comes out in its greenness and the flowers smile in their beauty, the dead will return from the Land of the Dead."

"Spring is too far off," sobbed Eagle. "It is only autumn now. I want my wife before spring. I want her just now."

"Well, come with me, and we will see if we can get her now," said Coyote.

Eagle wiped his tears away and picked up a basket. Then they started out for the Land of the Dead.

They traveled for a long time, until they came to a lake. Across it they could see houses, but there was no sign of people. Everything was as still as death.

"Oh! we have come all this way for nothing," wailed Eagle. "They are all dead here. I shall not find my wife."

"Wait until night, Brother Eagle," answered Coyote. "The dead sleep in the daytime. At night they come out. Let us rest until darkness falls." He threw himself down under a cypress tree, and Eagle lay down beside him.

When the sun had passed into the west, Coyote began to sing. He had sung only a short time, when four men came out of the houses across the lake and got into a canoe. Coyote sang on. The men did not touch the oars, but the boat skimmed over the water to the cypress tree.

Coyote and Eagle got into the canoe. Coyote kept on singing. The boat skimmed back over the water toward the houses. As it neared the shore, they heard music and drumming and dancing.

"What a good time the dead must have!" said Coyote. "I shall be glad to see them and their houses."

"You must not enter those houses," cautioned the four men in the boat. "You must not look at the people. This is a sacred place."

"But we are cold and hungry," replied Coyote. "Do let us in to warm ourselves."

"Well, you may come in for a little while," conceded the men.

They entered a large mat house. There were flowers in bloom and sweet music, and the people were all singing and dancing. Everybody looked well and happy.

An old woman came toward them. She carried a glass bottle in one hand and a feather in the other. "Eat, son," she said, and she dipped the feather into the bottle and passed it once over Coyote's tongue. He felt as well satisfied as if he had eaten a hearty meal.

"Eat, son," the old woman said again, and she let one dip of the feather fall into Eagle's mouth. His hunger, too, was satisfied.

Coyote and Eagle looked around them. They saw many of their dead friends. The friends did not answer them when they spoke, nor even look at them, but went on singing and dancing and having a happy time. Coyote saw that the mat house was lighted by the moon. The moon was hung from the ceiling, and the frog was attending to its light. As night faded, the spirit songs became fainter. By the time the sun appeared, all the dead had departed to sleep.

During the next day Coyote killed the frog and dressed himself in its clothes. Then at night he went into the mat house and attended to the light of the moon. All the dead people came again to the mat house. They began singing and dancing in a happy way. Suddenly Coyote swallowed the moon, and the mat house was in darkness. The spirit people began groping about. Coyote and Eagle picked them up and put them into the grass basket which they had brought from home. Then they shut the basket tight and started back to the Land of the Living.

Coyote carried the basket. After traveling a long while he heard a noise inside it. He pricked up his ears. "Brother Eagle," he said, "the people are beginnin‿ to come to life again."

Soon they heard different voices from the basket crying out, "I'm being bumped; I want to get out; I want to get out."

The basket was becoming very heavy. The nearer they came to the Land of the Living, the more alive the people became. They weighed nothing when they were spirits, but were heavy when they became alive. Coyote began to get tired carrying them. He said to Eagle, "Why not let them out as long as they wish to come?"

"No," answered Eagle; "let's get them home."

Still the voices from within grumbled and called aloud, "I want to get out ; I want to get out." Still the weight grew heavier with every step. Finally Coyote could not walk under it. He set the basket down.

"I am going to let them out," he said. "They are so far away from the Land of the Dead that they will not go back there now." He opened the basket. The dead people flew out. They changed into spirits and faded like the wind.

"Now," growled Eagle, "see what you 've done. You 'll have to go back with me in the spring, when the new buds are out, and try to get them back again."

"No," answered Coyote, "I 'm tired. The dead don't want to come back. They are happier in the Land of the Dead than we are in the Land of the Living. Let the dead stay in the Land of the Dead and never return to our land."

So because Coyote made this law, the dead do not come back. If he had not opened the basket, they would have returned every spring with the new grass and the fresh blossoms.

"Do you think my canary is singing now in the Land of the Dead, Klayukat ? "

"Yes, *Ninita*, he is singing all the night long."

"And is he happy, too?"

"Yes, *Chiquita*, happier than here."

"But who gives him seed and water and fresh chickweed?"

"The dead do not care about eating. They are happy without it. You may be sure your canary is happier than here."

"Oh, how lovely! You dear Klayukat! I must go and watch for Tonio. He'll be glad to have me tell him this story."

Klayukat looked after her. "*Pobrecita*," he murmured, and he sighed as he continued his stitching.

COYOTE'S RIDE ON A STAR

ONE day the children had been attempting to act *La Pastorela*, the sacred play which they saw presented every Christmas Eve at San Francisco. They found it easy to take the different parts in turn, but they had difficulty with the scenery. They had fashioned a star of sunflower petals, to represent the golden Star of Bethlehem, but the petals faded and curled up, and the star was not much of a success.

"Let's go to Wantasson. Perhaps he can fix us a star of real fire," proposed Juanita.

"Of course he can't," answered Antonio; "but we can ask him to do something for us."

"Make you a star?" and Wantasson removed his irons from the fire and sat down in the doorway. "I don't think I can make a star. A man would better leave stars alone. Think what the star did to Coyote."

"To Coyote? Why, what did a star do to Coyote?" and the children's interest was transferred from their play to the prospective story.

"Well, it was this way." Wantasson spread out his feet and rested his shoulders against the door, and then he began his story.

———

After Coyote had gotten fire and salmon for the animals and had destroyed their enemies, he began to feel proud of himself.

"I have more brains than any of the other animals," he said. "I ought to have more privileges than the rest of them."

Just then he noticed the stars glimmering above. "That's what I want," he thought, — "a ride on a star. All the other animals can walk on the earth, or run on it. I ought to have something better. I ought to have a journey on a star."

He went to the top of a hill and called to the evening star: "Come here, Bright Star. I want to take a ride on you."

The evening star only winked one eye and did not move any nearer.

"Did you hear me, O Star? I am the great Coyote. I have obtained heat and food for the animals, and have killed their destroyers. Now I want to journey around the world. Come nearer so that I can jump on you."

The evening star moved slowly away and smiled in silence.

At the next sundown Coyote mounted the hilltop again, and again called to the star. This time the evening star answered in the soft still voice that stars use on summer nights: "No, Coyote. You must remain on earth. Great as you are, you could not stand the pace of the stars."

But Coyote would not be content. Every night he whined and howled and craved and entreated, until at last the evening star became weary of his prayers.

"Well, jump on and be quick about it," it said, in the keen brisk voice that stars use in frost time.

It approached the hilltop a moment and then glided off. Coyote leaped and barely caught hold of it with his front paws. The star began whirling through space so fast that poor Coyote could not draw himself up onto its surface. He had to exert all his strength to hold on at all.

The star whirled along through the coldest regions. Coyote's paws became numb and frozen. At last they could not feel any longer, and he tumbled to the earth. It took him ten snows to get back, and then he fell so hard that he was flattened out as thin as a hazel bough.

Ever since his fall he has been thin, and every evening he goes up to the hilltop and reproaches the star for its harsh treatment.

"I think the evening star might have waited long enough to let him get comfortably on it," commented Juanita.

"So that's why the coyotes howl every night," observed Antonio. "I should think they'd be tired by this time."

"Oh, Coyote does not get tired. He is not like man. That is why man is so great — because Coyote did not get tired when he was making him."

"When Coyote was making man? Do you mean that Coyote made man?" The memory of his catechism weighted Antonio's word with doubt.

"Oh, have I not told you that story? No, I can't tell it now. Your Señor Padre wants these spurs fixed for this evening. You come to-morrow, and you will hear about it."

THE CREATION OF MAN

A S soon as their lessons were over in the morning, the children hastened to the blacksmith shop.

"Good morning, Wantasson. Are you ready to tell us how Coyote made man?"

"Good morning, children. Yes, a rest will do Wantasson good. Let us sit in the sun, and I will tell you the story now."

———

After Coyote had his great fall from the star, he sat around awhile doing nothing. Soon he grew tired of this and said, "I must do something."

He looked around the earth, but there was nothing to do. All the animals were warm and fat, and living without fear of anything. "They don't need any help," sighed Coyote, "but I must do something. I think I'll make a man."

136

He went down to the creek and began to model a figure out of the clay. As he worked, he became dissatisfied with the figure. "I wish I could make it better," he thought to himself. "I think I will ask the other animals for their opinions. Perhaps they can give me some good ideas."

He called all the animals of the world to meet together on the hilltop. The fishes wobbled up from the sea, the birds swept down from the heavens, and the other animals came hurrying from all the corners of the earth. They sat round in a circle, — Cougar, Grizzly, Antelope, Mountain Sheep, Deer, and so on, down to little Mouse, who was on the left of Cougar. In the center sat Coyote.

He said: "It is time for us to make man. Tell me how we shall make him."

"O-ho!" burst out Cougar. "That's easy. Give him a mighty voice to frighten all the animals, and long hair, and strong talons with terrible fangs at the end of them. Then he will be master of the world. O-ho!" and Cougar chuckled, as poor little Mouse shrunk away from him.

"Gru-u-u!" rumbled Grizzly. "It's perfectly ridiculous to have such a great voice. Half the time it frightens the prey so that it can hide. Give him a big enough voice, of course, but give him sense enough to seldom use it. Let him move quietly and swiftly. And let him have great strength to hold his capture."

"Huh!" wheezed Deer. "Strength to hold is good enough, but he would look foolish without antlers to fight with. I think, with Grizzly, that it is perfectly absurd to give him a roaring voice. I should pay less attention to his voice and more to his ears and eyes. Have his ears as sensitive as the spider's web, and his eyes like coals of fire. Then he can detect any approaching danger."

"Baa-aa!" bellowed Mountain Sheep. "Antlers are only a bother. They always catch in the brush. You would do better to roll up the antlers into little horns on either side of the forehead. That will give his head weight and enable him to butt harder."

"Oh, you animals have no brains," interrupted Coyote. "You each want man to be just like yourself. You might as well take one of your own children and call it *man*. Now you know that I am wiser than any of you, and yet I want man to be better than I am. Of course I wish him to have four legs like myself, and five toes. But Grizzly's toes spread out straight so that he can stand on two feet. That is a good thing. I want man's toes to be spread out like Grizzly's.

"Then, too, he'd better have no tail, like Grizzly, for tails are only good for fleas to ride on. He may

have a voice like Cougar's, but he need not roar all
the time. But as to giving him thick hair, that
would be a burden. Look at Fish. He is naked,
and he is comfortable under the hottest sun. So I
want man's skin to be like the skin of Fish. As to
claws, they should be like Eagle's, so that he can
carry things. Deer's eyes and ears are good, and
his throat, too. So I'd make man with ears and
eyes and throat like Deer's. His brains should be
like mine, so that he can rule the whole world."

"Nonsense! nonsense!" Beaver had been gur-
gling for some time. "No tail! no tail! Why, he
could not live without a good broad tail. How
would he haul his mud and build his house without
a tail?"

"And no wings?" hooted Owl. "No wings,
indeed! You are perfectly senseless not to think
of giving him wings."

"Pu-u-u!" sniffed Mole. "It's senseless to have
wings. They only bump you against the sky. And
eyes are useless, too. The sun only burns them.
It would be better to give him a soft fur, and let
him cuddle down in the moist, cool earth."

"Living in the earth is the worst nonsense of
all," exclaimed Mouse. "He will need to creep into
the sunshine to get warm. And he needs eyes to
see what he is eating."

"O-reech-o!" began Screech Owl, when Coyote ordered: "Stop your screeching. You may all go home. I 'll make man myself."

Each animal echoed, "I 'll make man myself," and they all rushed quarreling and snapping to the clay bank. Each began to model a figure.

At sundown they stopped to sleep,—all but Coyote. He went on working. When he heard snores from every bush, he went among the models of the other animals and destroyed every single one. Then he returned to his own figure and worked steadily. As the morning star mounted in the heavens, the figure of man was finished.

"Shine bright on him, O Morning Star!" whispered Coyote. "Give him life from the heavens, for he is to be superior to us all."

The morning star flashed five rays on the figure. Man straightened himself up. His eyes brightened. He stretched out his arms. Coyote took his hand and said: "You were partly made in the light, so you will always love the sunshine. You were partly made in the night, so you will never fear the darkness. Your mind will be active under sun or stars. You must gather cunning from all times, for henceforth you are to be the ruler of the world."

"But did n't Coyote feel sorry to have man the ruler of the world, when he had been the most cunning all along?" asked Antonio.

"Oh, Coyote! He does not mind about man. He and man are good friends. And he is more cunning now, for you know man made him more cunning."

"Man made him more cunning? How could man make Coyote more cunning?"

"I will tell you that story another time. Now I must heat my irons. Your Señor Padre will be in for dinner soon."

WHY THE COYOTE IS SO CUNNING

WHEN the children appeared at the smithy door the next day, Wantasson put down the irons he was handling.

"It is hard work being a blacksmith," he muttered, and he drew his sleeve across his brow.

"Well, rest awhile now, Wantasson," said Juanita, with sympathy in her voice and eyes.

"Would it tire you to tell how man made Coyote more cunning?" inquired Antonio.

"No, talking of Coyote does not tire me." He lounged into a comfortable position, sighed a few times, and then began the tale.

Up to the time man was made, all the animals were equal. It is true that Coyote was the wisest of them all, and the others looked to him for advice, but they all had equal rights to live and be happy on the face of the earth.

When man was created, he was superior to them all. Then he had to decide which animals should be considered strongest. He sat about making bows, one for each animal of the world and all of different lengths. He worked during every ray of light, but nine sleeps had passed before he had finished all the bows. Then he sent word to the animals that he would distribute the bows the next sunrise.

At sundown they gathered from far and near, every animal both great and small. When they had all settled themselves for sleep around the camp fire, Coyote thought to himself: "I am the wisest of the animals, so I ought to receive the longest bow. I think I will not sleep at all. Then I will be the first to greet man at sunrise."

It was hard to keep awake in such silence. Coyote rubbed his eyes and wriggled his toes. Still he felt sleepy. "I must skip around awhile, or I shall surely fall asleep," he murmured.

He jumped and skipped around the fire. The other animals began to waken. "Is it sunrise so soon?" yawned Grizzly.

"No. Go to sleep," whispered Coyote. "I was just getting a drink and stumbled over the tree root." To himself he said: "This will never do. If I move around, all the others will keep awake too. If I do not move around, I shall certainly fall asleep."

Just then the morning star peeped up over the hilltop. "I will watch her," said Coyote. "Her movements will keep me awake."

But the star traveled slowly, and his eyelids were weary of being open. "I know what I will do," and he sharpened two little sticks and put one in each eye to prop up his eyelids. "Now I will take a tiny nap, while my eyes are fixed on the star. When the sun comes up, the light in my open eyes will waken me."

The little nap grew into a sound sleep. Coyote's head lolled over on a manzanita bush. The sharp sticks in his eyes pierced right through the eyelids and kept them closed fast. Coyote slept on.

The morning star reached high in the sky. The leaves began to quiver. The birds called to each other their morning greetings. The animals stirred, rubbed their eyes, shook themselves, first slowly and then faster, and jumped to their feet facing the east. Still Coyote slept on.

As the sun stretched its golden fingers into the heavens, man appeared upon the hilltop. The animals clustered around him, all but Coyote, who still lay asleep unnoticed.

Man gave the first bow to Cougar, the second to Grizzly, and so on down the list, until he reached little stumpy Frog. After he had given Frog his,

"As the sun stretched its golden fingers into the heavens"

there was still one more bow left, the shortest of them all.

Man looked around. "What animal have I missed?" he asked. The animals glanced round their numbers. "Why, Coyote is not here!" said Cougar.

Away they all scampered to search for him. Soon they found him, fast asleep, with his head on the manzanita branch. They danced on him and shouted: "Oh, hi, Coyote! Wake up! wake up! You have the shortest bow. You're not so strong as little squatty Frog. Oh, hi, Coyote! Coyote! Ha, ha!"

Coyote sat up dazed. The sticks held his eyelids shut fast. He could not see, but he could feel the sunshine; and the laughs of the animals maddened him.

He pulled the stick out of his right eye, then the one from his left. He blinked his eyes. Yes, there were all the animals, each with a bow. Only a tiny little bow was left at man's feet. Coyote put his head down between his paws and wept.

Man felt sorry for him, and said to the animals: "You should not laugh at him. He has helped you many a day. As I cannot make him the strongest animal, I will give him ten times his former cunning."

Then Coyote lifted up his head and looked his thanks into man's eyes.

Ever since that day Coyote has not been the strongest of the animals; but he is, as he was before, the most cunning and the wisest. And to this day he is a friend of man and never hurts one of man's children.

———

"Were n't those animals horrid to laugh at him, when he had been so good to them?" and Juanita's eyes flamed with indignation.

"Yes, I'm glad that he's still the most cunning. And he never hurt a man, did he, Wantasson?"

"No, young Antonio. Never did he, and never will he. But there is that Tecla coming this way. You go to her. I must return to my work," and the party dispersed.

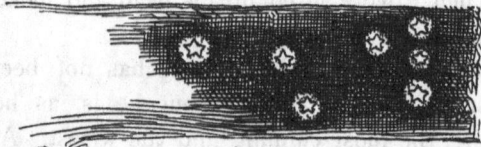

THE STORY OF THE PLEIADES

THE children's father had showed them a map of the heavens in an old astronomy that had belonged to their great-grandfather. He had also pointed out certain groups in the sky and had told them the old stories connected with each. They were charmed with their new knowledge, and night after night they insisted on indicating the Dipper, Orion, Cassiopeia's Chair, and the Pleiades, and repeating by turns the myth of each.

One day they were discussing the story of the Pleiades near the blacksmith shop. Wantasson stood at his door and listened to them.

"Ugh!" he muttered. "My people have a better story than that about the seven sisters, — a better story."

"Oh, have you a story about the seven sisters, Wantasson?" and the two children were at his side, eager to listen.

"Yes, we have seven sisters up in the sky, too, but they are not the seven sisters you children were just talking about."

Wantasson sank to the doorsill and fixed himself comfortably.

Many, many rains ago, when the earth was still in its infancy, seven brothers wedded seven sisters, and they all lived in one little village together. Socoy, the oldest brother, married Fosate, the eldest sister; Vichili, the second brother, married the second sister, Alachu; and so on they mated, according to their ages, — Stapocono and Moquem; Chapac and Yacumu; Sauset and Ajalis; Canuya and Tacchel; until the youngest brother, Tucay, took unto himself the youngest sister, the radiant Lilote.

In the daytime the seven brothers climbed the hills together, hunting game, while the seven sisters went together down to the lake basin to dig roots.

Every evening, as the sun withdrew to his council with the creators, the sisters returned home. Their shoulders were bent low with loads of lily roots. Always they found the seven brothers at home before them, lying around the fire, with tongues eager to explain the lack of game. Night after night the six oldest brothers had nothing for their wives. Tucay alone each sundown produced a rabbit for his Lilote. In silence the sisters roasted their roots and shared them with their husbands.

This experience was repeated daily for eight moons. Then the sisters began to grumble among themselves. Fosate, the eldest, said: "This will not do. My bones are rattling in my skin. I want flesh food. We must think of something to do to save ourselves."

The next morning the seven husbands took their bows and arrows and went to meet the sun. Then Fosate said to her youngest sister: "Lilote, you must stay here to-day. Hide yourself behind the willows, and when our husbands come home, watch what they do. Then you can tell them that you stayed at home because you had a pain in your face."

When the sun was smiling its broadest, Lilote heard the brothers returning. She hid herself behind the willows. Laughing, each man threw down two rabbits and busied himself renewing the fire. As the flames changed the wood into coals, they skinned their prey. Tucay chose the larger of his rabbits and laid it to one side.

Thereupon Socoy, his eldest brother, laughed at him. "O stupid Tucay! to stint yourself, when your Lilote knows nothing of your success! We men need the flesh to give us great strength. It is a woman's place to deny herself for us."

The five other brothers argued in the same strain. Tucay answered each time: "You do what you like. I wish to save half of my game for my wife."

"And the better half at that," scoffed Socoy; and all the others joined in teasing their youngest brother.

Lilote behind the willows heard and saw all. Her heart quickened as she listened to Tucay's words. Her mouth watered when the rabbit legs sizzled on the hot coals, but she kept as still as the quail in the thicket.

The brothers licked their lips in satisfaction over the last morsels, and hid the bones and skins in the gulch below the village. Then they settled around the fire to smoke.

In a little while Lilote came noisily out of her own hut. She rubbed her eyes and yawned broadly. Her face was bound up in cascara leaves. As she saw the brothers, she stopped in apparent surprise. "Are you home so soon, or have I slept all day? I had a pain in my face this morning and did not go out. How much game did you get?"

She seemed sleepy and unsuspicious. The brothers asked a few questions, and then believed that she knew nothing of their feast.

When the sisters returned that night, there was the same old story of no game. Then in silence they roasted their roots and shared them with their husbands. As Lilote watched the men eat, she thought: "These must surely be gopher snakes. No man could eat a meal so soon after their gorging."

When the brothers settled around the fire again and began smoking, the sisters crept behind the willows. There Lilote whispered the story of their husbands' treachery.

"Let us steal down to the lake," murmured Fosate, "and there think what to do."

Down along the stream's bank they stole without a word. When they reached the shore of the lake, they huddled together in the darkness.

Fosate declared: "We must do something to get away from these greedy men. What shall we do?"

"Let us change ourselves into water," suggested Alachu, the second sister.

"Oh, no! They would drink us," the others answered.

"Let us change ourselves into stone," said Moquem, the third sister.

"Oh, no! They would step on us," came the response.

"Let us turn ourselves into trees," recommended Yacumu, the fourth sister.

"Oh, no! They would burn us," was the chorus.

"Let us change ourselves into quails," advised Ajalis, the fifth sister.

"Oh, no! They would shoot us," the others replied.

"Let us turn ourselves into stars," said Tacchel, the sixth sister.

"Oh, no! They would look at us," rang out five voices.

But Lilote said: "Yes, let us change ourselves into stars. Then we shall be out of reach."

"And we can watch them hunt for us," added Tacchel. This decided the sisters. Stars they would be.

They said to the tules on the lake's brink: "O tules! give us your aid. We wish a boat lighter and swifter than any canoe. We want to sail into the very heavens, away from these greedy husbands."

They fashioned the tules into a boat and carried it to a high point of rock. Then they stepped into it and rowed off into space. When they were far enough away, they got out and sat together in a group in the sky. Then they let the tule boat glide back to earth.

From their seat on high they watched their husbands. The six oldest brothers looked around a little while and then settled back to smoke by the fire. But Tucay, the youngest, wandered around wailing. "My wife, my fair Lilote," he cried, "come again and warm my heart. No more shall I follow the advice of my brothers. You shall have all that I slay. Come, Lilote, come, or I perish in this loneliness."

Lilote watched his misery for a day and a night. Then she declared: "I shall throw myself back to earth. I cannot leave him so."

"And would you not grieve for us?" inquired Fosate.

"We will never go back," cried the other sisters. "O little one! do not desert us."

Lilote endured her husband's sorrow for another day and another night. Then she said, "I must go back, sisters, although I shall ever grieve over your absence."

"No, little one," answered Fosate. "You will stay here, and we will bring your beloved to you. He has proved himself worthy of our companionship."

All the sisters agreed to this, and they told Tucay how to use the tule boat. He came speeding up to them, and they changed him into the constellation Taurus.

You can still see them sitting in the high heavens, the Pleiades and Taurus, always in happy companionship and ever watching over the loyal lovers of this world.

———

"Oh, I'm so glad they took up Tucay. You wouldn't eat all the rabbits and give me none, would you, Tonio?" and Juanita pressed her head against her brother's arm.

"No, *Ninita mia.*" Antonio moved himself free. "I'd get the rabbits, and you'd get the roots, and we would build a big fire as they do at the barbecues, and roast them. Let's play barbecue now. I'll go back of the corral and make a fire. You can go and ask Maria for a piece of meat. And get some figs. They'll do for roots," and Antonio started off.

"Aha, Tonito! So Juanita will be bringing both the rabbit and the roots. You're worse than the six brothers," and Wantasson chuckled as the children sped away to their play.

GLOSSARY OF CALIFORNIA TERMS

Abalone: a shellfish found on the Pacific coast, having an iridescent shell.

Adobe: originally the sun-baked bricks; also applied to buildings built of these bricks.

Barbecue: the roasting of a whole animal in a pit, — the principal feature of many a festivity.

Cascara sagrada: a medicinal plant whose value is now appreciated by the whole world. Tons of the bark are shipped from California annually.

Chiquita: a diminutive of endearment.

La Fiesta del Señor: Christmas Day.

Lagunita: a little lake.

La Pastorela: a play performed at all the Spanish-Californian settlements on Christmas Eve. It represented the story of the Nativity and of the triumph of the Faith over the wiles of Satan.

Madre: mother.

Mission San Francisco d'Assisi: the foundation of the present city of San Francisco.

Ninita mia: "my little girl," a very common term of endearment.

Padre: father.

Pobrecita: " poor little one," commonly used to-day.

Quadrangle: the Spanish-Californian homes of the better class were built in the shape of a quadrangle, with a central court.

Ripe olives: the ripe olives are those which are not picked from the trees until they are mature. They are pickled in brine, just as the green unripe olives are, but are as much more delicious as is a ripe plum than an unripe one.

Señor: sir.

Tortillas: unleavened cakes of Indian corn or of wheat baked on the coals.

Tules: water reeds.

Whalebone: the vertebræ of the whale were used to pave streets and yards. A vertebra was often used as a seat.

INDEX

Abalone, 69

Acorn, 22

Adobe, 32, 47

Alder, 92

Alta California, vii, 4

Ant, 31–33

Antelope, 13, 137

Ash, 9

Awl, 80, 81, 104

Baby-blue-eyes, 12

Baja California, vii, 4

Bat, 114–117

Bear, 26

Beaver, 13, 50, 96–99, 139

Blacksmith, 23, 33

Blue Jay, 48–50, 53–54, 63, 64,
    66, 67, 68, 69

Brass buttons, 5, 22

Buttercups, 12

Canary, 125, 130, 131

Cascara, 47, 151

Cassiopeia's Chair, 148

Cat, 32, 74

Cedar, 9, 193

Chaparral, 12

Chicken Hawk, 53

Clam, 68–69

Cloud, 31–32

Coffee berry, 12

Colors, 63–69

Cottonwood, 92

Cougar, 13, 35–37, 137, 144, 146

Coyote, 5–6, 7–13, 15–20, 25–29,
    38–41, 56–57, 95–99, 100–104,
    109–113, 118–124, 125–131,
    132–135, 136–141, 142–147

Crab apple, 39, 40–41

Crane, 82–83, 90–91, 115, 116

Cricket, 34–37

Crow, 91

Cypress, 127

Daughters of Blue Jay, 65–69

Deer, 76–83, 101, 102, 104, 137,
    138, 139

Dipper, the, 148

Dog, 13, 32, 74

Dog Star, 54

Eagle, 9–13, 44–45, 126–130,
    139

Elder, 39, 40, 98

Elk, 28, 89, 101

Epiphany, 75

159

Feather, 110, 111
Fig trees, 105
Fir, 12, 93
Fire, 25–29, 32–33, 93, 115, 116
Fish, 137, 139
Flea, 37
Flint, 17, 19
Fox, 28, 57
Frog, 5–6, 21–22, 28–29, 59–61,
   128, 129, 144, 146

Good Kings, 74, 75
Great Bear, 54
Grizzly, 13, 76–83, 137, 138, 143

Hawk, 16–19
Hazel, 39, 40, 85, 134

Jack Rabbit, 105–108

Knife, 33

La Fiesta del Señor, 74
Land, 9–12
Land of the Dead, 125–131
Lark, 49, 61
Lizard, 115–116
Loon, 53
Lower California, vii, 4

Man, 135, 136–141, 142–147
Man-of-tar, 70–74
Manzanita, 12, 144, 146
Maple, 92
Mole, 139

Moon, 19–20, 56–58, 59–61, 128,
   129
Mosquito, 37, 38–42
Mountain sheep, 101, 137, 138
Mountains, 12
Mouse, 32, 52–53, 137, 139

Nightingale, 49

Oak, 5, 21, 40, 41
Orion, 148
Owl, 53, 113, 118–124, 139, 140
Ox, 33

Panther, 26
Pine, 12, 39, 41
Pleiades, 148–155
Poppies, 12
Potentilla, 65, 66

Rabbit, 105–108
Raccoon, 70–74
Rat, 52–53
Rattlesnake, 43–46
Redwood, 12
Robin, 49, 52, 85–94

Salmon, 95–99
Salmon Berry, 85–90
Serpents, 12–13
Seven sisters, 148–155
Sickness, 11
Skate, 49–50
Skunk, 50–52
Snow, 31

Southwest wind, 47–55
Squirrel, 28, 74
Star, 132–135, 140, 144, 148–155
Stick, 32
Sun, 15–19, 31, 105–108, 144
Sunflower, 8, 111, 132

Taurus, 155
Three Wise Kings, 75
Thrush, 49
Thunder, 109–113, 114

Tick, 100–104
Tules, 17, 19, 153, 154
Turkey, 53

Vine maple, 93

Water, 33
Whip-poor-will, 60–61
Willow, 91–92
Wind, 32, 47–55, 116
Witch, 44–46
Wren, 49